THE LAYMAN'S BIBLE COMMENTARY

THE LAYMAN'S BIBLE COMMENTARY
IN TWENTY-FIVE VOLUMES

THE LAYMAN'S
BIBLE COMMENTARY

Balmer H. Kelly, *Editor*
Donald G. Miller   *Associate Editors*   Arnold B. Rhodes
Dwight M. Chalmers, *Editor, John Knox Press*

VOLUME 7

THE FIRST AND SECOND BOOKS OF THE
KINGS

THE FIRST AND SECOND BOOKS OF THE
CHRONICLES

Robert C. Dentan

JOHN KNOX PRESS
ATLANTA, GEORGIA

10 9 8 7 6 5 4 3 2

Complete set: ISBN: 0-8042-3086-2
This volume: 0-8042-3067-6
Library of Congress Card Number: 59-10454
First paperback edition 1982
Printed in the United States of America
John Knox Press
Atlanta, Georgia 30365

PREFACE

The LAYMAN'S BIBLE COMMENTARY is based on the conviction that the Bible has the Word of good news for the whole world. The Bible is not the property of a special group. It is not even the property and concern of the Church alone. It is given to the Church for its own life but also to bring God's offer of life to all mankind—wherever there are ears to hear and hearts to respond.

It is this point of view which binds the separate parts of the LAYMAN'S BIBLE COMMENTARY into a unity. There are many volumes and many writers, coming from varied backgrounds, as is the case with the Bible itself. But also as with the Bible there is a unity of purpose and of faith. The purpose is to clarify the situations and language of the Bible that it may be more and more fully understood. The faith is that in the Bible there is essentially one Word, one message of salvation, one gospel.

The LAYMAN'S BIBLE COMMENTARY is designed to be a concise non-technical guide for the layman in personal study of his own Bible. Therefore, no biblical text is printed along with the comment upon it. This commentary will have done its work precisely to the degree in which it moves its readers to take up the Bible for themselves.

The writers have used the Revised Standard Version of the Bible as their basic text. Occasionally they have differed from this translation. Where this is the case they have given their reasons. In the main, no attempt has been made either to justify the wording of the Revised Standard Version or to compare it with other translations.

The objective in this commentary is to provide the most helpful explanation of fundamental matters in simple, up-to-date terms. Exhaustive treatment of subjects has not been undertaken.

In our age knowledge of the Bible is perilously low. At the same time there are signs that many people are longing for help in getting such knowledge. Knowledge of and about the Bible is, of course, not enough. The grace of God and the work of the Holy Spirit are essential to the renewal of life through the Scriptures. It is in the happy confidence that the great hunger for the Word is a sign of God's grace already operating within men, and that the Spirit works most wonderfully where the Word is familiarly known, that this commentary has been written and published.

THE EDITORS AND
THE PUBLISHERS

THE FIRST AND SECOND BOOKS OF THE
KINGS

THE FIRST AND SECOND BOOKS OF THE
CHRONICLES

INTRODUCTION

In a profound sense, the whole Bible is a book of history. From one point of view it can be regarded as the history of the wonderful works of God; from another it is the history of God's people—seen first as the nation of Israel and then as the Christian Church. In the Books of Kings and Chronicles it is this second aspect—the history of the *people* of God—which is primary. These books tell us the story of Israel's life during a long and very significant epoch, an epoch nearly four centuries long, which saw the nation gradually decline from a united, wealthy kingdom, ruling over an empire of its own, to an impoverished and desolated province of one of the great empires of the heathen world. At the beginning of First Kings, Jerusalem is a proud capital city, in the process of being beautified by lavish expenditures; at the end of Second Kings (and Second Chronicles also) it is a heap of ruins, its walls destroyed, its great buildings burned, and its population carried off into exile (II Kings 25:9-11; II Chron. 36:19-20).

If these books stood by themselves, the story they have to tell could only be regarded as a tragic one and we should read them merely out of curiosity about the sad fate of an ancient people. But set as they are in the context of the whole Bible story, we can see that the episodes they relate were a part of God's ongoing work with the human race, a necessary part of the religious and moral education of his people. This part of the story is not simply the account of a people's decline from power to impotence; it is rather the narrative of how a people lost its life in order to find it again. For the true greatness of the people of Israel is not to be found in the glories of Solomon's court, with

which the Books of Kings begin, but rather in the spiritual
achievements of the great religious teachers who lived during the
nation's declining years. They saw God's hand at work in the
catastrophic events of their time and bequeathed to later generations the profound insight into the nature of God and man
which they gained in those evil days. This heritage is preserved
for us in the Books of Amos, Hosea, Isaiah, Micah, Zephaniah,
Habakkuk, Jeremiah, and Ezekiel. All of these prophets lived
during the period covered by First and Second Kings and First
and Second Chronicles, and their teaching is hardly intelligible
unless seen against the historical background which these books
provide. The prophetic interpretation of life, which is Israel's
greatest achievement, is thus the product of her deepest travail.
This is the paradox which the whole Bible teaches—that we
lose in order to gain, that through weakness we become strong,
that God frequently chooses the road to defeat as the road to
victory. No books speak more eloquently of this theme than the
Books of Kings and Chronicles when seen in relationship to
other books of the Bible and in the context of the whole story
of the People of God.

The Character of the Books of the Kings

As the name implies, the Books of the Kings, which constitute
a single work divided only for convenience into two volumes,
deal with a major part of the history of the two kingdoms of
Judah and Israel. The beginning of the Hebrew monarchy under the first two kings, Saul and David, is related in the two
books we call First and Second Samuel. In the Greek version
of the Old Testament (the Septuagint) these four books are all
grouped together under a single name, I-IV Kingdoms, a fact
which conveniently indicates their close relationship and over-all
subject. Taken together, Samuel and Kings provide us with a
full history of the time when kings bore rule in ancient Israel.
(We may note, by anticipation, that First and Second Chronicles
cover the same period, though with a different perspective and
a different set of interests.)

Neither Samuel nor Kings were originally conceived as independent books, but rather they came into being as part of the
long consecutive history of the people of Israel which begins with
the Book of Deuteronomy and ends with Second Kings and

therefore covers all the significant events from the time of Moses down to the final collapse of the Hebrew kingdoms. This long history is often called the "Deuteronomic" history because the authors of it were influenced by the philosophy of the Book of Deuteronomy and the great reform of Josiah, with which (as we shall see) Deuteronomy obviously had some kind of connection. This Deuteronomic history consists of Deuteronomy, Joshua, Judges, Samuel, and Kings. (Ruth, which now interrupts the series, does not belong in this position and is found elsewhere in the Hebrew Bible.) All of these books have the same understanding of the principles which determine the course of history, and all make frequent use of a style of writing which is rarely found elsewhere and which occurs in its most concentrated form in the Book of Deuteronomy.

No writer of history in the Bible was concerned simply with recording facts and events in their proper order and sequence. All were concerned to show some *meaning* in history, to show how God is at work among men and how nations rise and fall in obedience to God's plan and to the operation of an inexorable moral law. Since men can quite legitimately find more than one meaning in any series of historical events, an author, if he wishes to be clear, must take a definite point of view and select for his record those events or aspects of events which most clearly illustrate the principles which he sees at work. To some extent this is true of all writers of history both ancient and modern. So, to understand any historical work, it is of first importance to understand the author's point of view. Fortunately the Deuteronomic historians had a point of view which was unmistakable and which dominates the whole Deuteronomic history. They believed that Yahweh, the God of Israel, had instructed his people in a certain way of life and a manner of worship which they were obligated to follow with undeviating loyalty. When they did so, they were happy and prosperous in the land which he had given them; when they turned away from it, they met with disaster. The giving of God's law is recorded in the Book of Deuteronomy, chapter 28 of that book containing the most complete statement of the Deuteronomic philosophy; the giving of the land is recorded in the Book of Joshua; the story of Israel's recurrent, ungrateful failure to obey God's law is told in the following books—Judges, Samuel, and Kings—culminating at last in the loss of the land, the destruction of Israel's political life, and the exile of her people to a foreign country. It is a grim lesson which First and Second Kings have to teach when seen as a part of the complete Deuteronomic history; but, of course, it has a very different aspect when seen in the framework of the Bible story as a whole. And, as we shall see, the Deuteronomic historians have their cheerful side as well. If the facts of history compel them to teach their lesson chiefly in negative terms, it is none the less true that the message is fundamentally a positive one. The lesson they wished to teach was not so much that catastrophe is the result of disobedience as that prosperity and happiness are the sure reward of those who love God and obey him.

The date of the Deuteronomic history, including Kings, can be fairly determined by the last events which it mentions. Since the last date recorded is 561 B.C. (II Kings 25:27), midway through the period of the Babylonian Exile, we may assume the books were fixed in their present form shortly after that. There is some evidence that an earlier form of the Books of Kings, with a more optimistic point of view, had been issued during the heyday of King Josiah's reform, between 621 and 609 B.C. This edition would have ended with II Kings 23:25. Sometime during the early years of the Babylonian Exile this was brought up to date by adding II Kings 23:26—25:21, which tells the story of Josiah's death and the fall of Jerusalem, and by revising some of the early parts to bring out more clearly the lesson that the Exile was a punishment for Israel's sins. Finally, when the Exile had lasted more than a quarter of a century, another hand added the two concluding paragraphs of the present book, which briefly recount the unhappy events immediately following the destruction of the kingdom (II Kings 25:22-26) and tell of an incident which seemed to point toward a renewal of God's favor toward his people in the future (see the comment on II Kings 25:27-30). It is obvious that neither the original author (or authors?) nor the later editors of the Deuteronomic history lived to see the return of Israel from exile in 538 B.C. and the re-establishment of her life on her native soil.

While the Deuteronomic historians who produced the Books of Kings were chiefly concerned with using history to teach certain religious and moral principles, they were remarkably careful and objective in using the sources of information at their disposal. Most of the time they were content simply to quote from their source or to summarize it and then add their own comments at the end. So, in effect, Kings appears as a kind of patchwork quilt, made up of quotations from a number of different ancient documents, of rather differing quality and value, connected by a thread of moralizing comment. Several of the sources used are mentioned by name: "the book of the acts of Solomon" (I Kings 11:41), "the Chronicles of the Kings of Judah" (I Kings 14:29), "the Chronicles of the Kings of Israel" (I Kings 15:31). The way in which these sources are referred to shows that our authors used only excerpts, largely chosen to suit their purpose in writing, but it also shows that they intended to write reliable history which could be checked by reference to the original documents. In addition to the sources explicitly mentioned, we may infer that they also made use of several other documents: historical records of a more informal character, official records of the Temple, and, of especial importance, popular lives of the prophets Elijah and Elisha. It was a complex task which these historians of ancient Israel set for themselves, and, considering the specifically religious purpose for which they wrote, they carried it out with remarkable skill and in a surprisingly scientific spirit.

The Character of the Books of the Chronicles

One must warn the reader at the outset against confusing the biblical Books of Chronicles with "the Chronicles of the Kings of Judah" and "of Israel" mentioned in the preceding paragraph. The similarity of names is purely coincidental. The latter were official records written and preserved by public recorders at the royal court and were presumably destroyed at the fall of Jerusalem. The *books* of Chronicles are part of a later work of history which rewrote from a different point of view the story recorded in Samuel and Kings and was probably intended by the author to replace the older works.

As one cannot properly appreciate the Books of Kings unless he sees them as a part of the larger Deuteronomic history, one cannot understand the two Books of Chronicles unless he is aware that they are part of a comprehensive work on world history in four volumes, "Chronicles" constituting volumes one and two and "Ezra" and "Nehemiah" volumes three and four. If one notes the mention of Adam in I Chronicles 1:1, he will see that ideally the "Chronicler" (as, for convenience, we call the author of this great work) intended to produce a compendium of world history down to his own time. Since the last high priest he mentions is Jaddua (Neh. 12:11), who is known to have been a contemporary of Alexander the Great, we must assume that the author lived shortly after that time, probably in the early third century (300-200) B.C. In other words, he compiled his history at least two hundred years after the Books of Kings were written.

His work is very different from the Deuteronomic history in scope, method, and philosophical outlook. The differences need to be seen in sharp contrast: The Deuteronomic history covers the period from Moses to the fall of Jerusalem; the Chronicler's history covers the period from Adam to the rebuilding of Jerusalem and the work of Ezra and Nehemiah. The Deuteronomic historians had a definite point of view, but were scrupulous in reproducing their sources; the Chronicler was much less precise in his use of the sources. He was more concerned that his story should be religiously edifying than that it be merely historically accurate. Since his principal sources were our own Books of Samuel and Kings, we can easily see, by comparison, how he deals with them. He omits stories that he considers discreditable to his characters, for instance, the David and Bathsheba episode and the whole account of Absalom's rebellion against his father; he leaves out the entire history of the northern kingdom of Israel, since it was irrelevant to his purpose and he considered Israel a wicked and apostate kingdom; he makes his story more interesting and gives to it a more directly religious tone by introducing miraculous incidents where there are none in the original (compare, for example, I Kings 8:54-56 with II Chron. 7:1-3). Occasionally he alters the theology of a passage (notably in I Chron. 21:1 as compared with II Sam. 24:1). These facts make it evident that he was much more of a theologian than a scientific historian in the modern sense. Finally, we must note that his purpose and field of interest were quite different from those of the older historians. They were primarily moralists, interested in illustrating the working out of the moral law in the history of the People of God; he was a churchman, chiefly interested in the Temple and its services and in showing how the building of the Temple under David and Solomon and its rebuilding under Zerubbabel were the central events in the history of Israel, if not of the whole world.

Because of the Chronicler's interest in the Temple, its worship and especially its music, it has been inferred, and probably correctly, that he was a Levite, a member of one of the Temple choirs. (Notice, for instance, how he introduces the Levites and Temple singers into the story of David's bringing the Ark to Jerusalem; compare II Sam. 6:13-15 with I Chron. 15:26-28.) For this reason his book has unique value, giving us a rare glimpse into the mentality of those who served the Temple and helping us to understand the background of the Psalms, many of which were probably produced by the same group. (Note, for example, the mention of Asaph in the title of Psalm 50 and also in I Chron. 16:4-5.) The book, incidentally, contains some fine examples of ancient liturgical prayer, such as I Chronicles 29:10-19. No other book in the Bible, aside from the Psalter itself, gives us so vivid a sense of what the Temple and its regularly appointed acts of praise, prayer, penitence, and thanksgiving could mean to the ancient Hebrew worshiper.

From what has been said, the reader may conclude that Chronicles has only negligible historical value, great as may be its importance for other purposes. In part this is true. Where the Chronicler has simply rewritten the text of Samuel and Kings, we can see that his motive in most cases was not greater historical accuracy, but rather to explain things which seemed difficult, to remove things which seemed unedifying or immoral, and to make God's part in the story more explicit. In passages where the Chronicler is directly dependent on Samuel or Kings, it seems clear that greater credence is to be given to the older historians. Nevertheless, there are a number of passages in Chronicles which have no parallel in the Deuteronomic history and in which the specific interests of the Chronicler do not appear. In such places the author may well have had access to records which were not available to the authors of Samuel and Kings. While this material must be treated with a certain caution in view of what we know of the Chronicler's historical method elsewhere, it is at least possible that we have here some important supplementary data on the history of the Hebrew monarchy. Such a passage as II Chronicles 17:10-19 would, if its information is accurate, add a good deal to our knowledge of the reign of Jehoshaphat, otherwise so meagerly reported in I Kings 22:41-50.

In conclusion, however, it must be emphasized again that the chief value of the Books of Chronicles is not so much in the history they relate as in the insight they give into the mind of the author and the spirit of the times in which he lived. The Books of

Kings are the product of a school of moralists and historians, disciples of the great Hebrew prophets; the Books of Chronicles are the product of a poet, a churchman and a devotee of the liturgy, a follower of the priests and the Levites. With some obvious allowances, we may say that in reading the Books of Kings we are like the audience in a motion-picture theater watching the selected scenes of a newsreel and listening to the voice of a commentator; when we read Chronicles we are rather like a congregation in a great church studying the same scenes as they are represented in a series of stained-glass windows. While we may be more attracted to the one method of presentation than to the other, it can hardly be denied that both are important ways of representing and interpreting the truth and each is able to convey aspects which are not easily preserved in any other fashion.

The Relationship Between the Books of the Kings and the Books of the Chronicles

The following table shows the general interrelationship of Kings and Chronicles and indicates the span of history covered by these books.

Adam to Saul (mostly genealogies and lists)		I Chron. 1-9
The United Monarchy (Saul, David, and Solomon)	(I Samuel 31— I Kings 11)	I Chron. 10— II Chron. 9
The Death of Saul	(I Samuel 31)	I Chron. 10
The Reign of David	(II Samuel 1-24)	I Chron. 11-29
David's Death and Its Consequences	I Kings 1-2	I Chron. 29:22b-30
The Reign of Solomon	I Kings 3-11	II Chron. 1-9
The Divided Kingdoms	I Kings 12— II Kings 17 (+18:9-12)	II Chron. 10-28 (the history of Judah only)
The Remaining History of Judah	II Kings 18:1—25:21	II Chron. 29:1—36:21
Events During the Exile	II Kings 25:22-30	
Cyrus' Decree for Rebuilding the Temple	(Ezra 1:1-3a)	II Chron. 36:22-23

While it is difficult to break down into smaller units the part of Kings which deals with the divided kingdoms because of the editors' complex method of interweaving the histories of Judah and Israel, it will be useful to note the way in which Kings and Chronicles are interrelated with respect to the history of *the kings of Judah.*

Rehoboam	I Kings 12:1-24; 14:21-31	II Chron. 10-12
Abijah (called Abijam in Kings)	15:1-8	13
Asa	15:9-24	14-16
Jehoshaphat	22:1-50	17-20
Jehoram	II Kings 8:16-24	21
Ahaziah	8:25-29; 9:21-29	22:1-9
Athaliah	11	22:10— 23:21
Joash	12	24
Amaziah	14:1-14, 17-22	25
Uzziah (called Azariah in Kings)	15:1-7	26
Jotham	15:32-38	27
Ahaz	16	28
Hezekiah	18-20	29-32
Manasseh	21:1-18	33:1-20
Amon	21:19-26	33:21-25
Josiah	22:1—23:30	34-35
Jehoahaz	23:31-35	36:1-4
Jehoiakim	23:36—24:7	36:5-8
Jehoiachin	24:8-17; 25:27-30	36:9-10
Zedekiah	24:18— 25:21	36:11-12

We must note also the names of *the kings of Israel* and those sections of the Books of Kings which deal with them (there is no account of the history of the Northern Kingdom in Chronicles):

Jeroboam I	I Kings 12:1— 14:20
Nadab, Baasha, Elah, Zimri, and Omri	15:25— 16:28
Ahab	16:29— 22:40
Ahaziah	22:51— II Kings 1:18
Jehoram	2:1—8:15; 9:1—10:28
Jehu	10:29-36
Jehoahaz	13:1-9
Jehoash	13:10-25; 14:15-16
Jeroboam II	14:23-29

Zechariah, Shallum,
  Menahem, Pekahiah,
  and Pekah
	15:8-31

Hoshea	17:1-23; 18:9-12

With the fall of Hoshea, the last of the northern kings, a mixed people called the Samaritans were brought in to take the place of the Israelites. This story is related in II Kings 17:24-41.

Finally, it may be noted that the narratives about Elijah and Elisha, which constitute so important a part of these books, are interspersed throughout the sections of these books dealing with the reigns of the northern kings from Ahab to Jehoash, beginning with the first appearance of Elijah in I Kings 17:1 and ending with the death of Elisha in II Kings 13:14-21.

OUTLINE

David's Death and Its Consequences. I Kings 1:1—2:46
The King's Illness and Solomon's Accession (I Kings 1:1-53)
David's Death and Solomon's Consolidation of Power (I Kings 2:1-46)

The Reign of Solomon. I Kings 3:1—11:43
Preamble (I Kings 3:1-28)
Solomon, Organizer of the Kingdom (I Kings 4:1-28)
Solomon, the Patron of Culture (I Kings 4:29-34)
Solomon, the Builder (I Kings 5:1—9:25)
Solomon, the Merchant Prince (I Kings 9:26—10:29)
The Dark Side of Solomon's Reign (I Kings 11:1-40)
The Death of Solomon (I Kings 11:41-43)

The History of the Divided Kingdoms.
I Kings 12:1—II Kings 17:41
The Revolt of Northern Israel (I Kings 12:1-24)
The Reign of Jeroboam I in Israel (I Kings 12:25—14:20)
The Disastrous Reign of Rehoboam in Judah (I Kings 14:21-31)
The Short Reign of Abijam in Judah (I Kings 15:1-8)
The Reforming Reign of Asa in Judah (I Kings 15:9-24)
The Brief Reign of Nadab in Israel (I Kings 15:25-32)
The Reigns of Baasha, Elah, and Zimri in Israel (I Kings 15:33—16:22)
The Important Reign of Omri in Israel (I Kings 16:23-28)
The Critical Reign of Ahab in Israel (I Kings 16:29—22:40)
The Good Reign of Jehoshaphat in Judah (I Kings 22:41-50)
The Insignificant Reign of Ahaziah in Israel (I Kings 22:51—II Kings 1:18)
The Crucial Reign of Jehoram in Israel (II Kings 2:1—8:15)
The Reign of Jehoram in Judah (II Kings 8:16-24)
The Reign of Ahaziah in Judah (II Kings 8:25-29)
The Revolution of Jehu (II Kings 9:1—10:28)
The Unsatisfactory Reign of Jehu in Israel (II Kings 10:29-36)
The Evil Reign of Athaliah in Judah (II Kings 11:1-21)
The Reign of Jehoash in Judah (II Kings 12:1-21)

The Remaining History of the Kingdom of Judah.

Appendix: Events During the Exile. II Kings 25:22-30

COMMENTARY

DAVID'S DEATH AND ITS CONSEQUENCES
I Kings 1:1—2:46

The King's Illness and Solomon's Accession (1:1-53)

The Beginning of David's Last Sickness (1:1-4)

The first two chapters of First Kings are a continuation of the story of David's reign as told in the Books of Samuel and are probably derived from the same original document. This early source is one of the most valuable historical records preserved in our Bible and is perhaps to be regarded as the prose masterpiece of the Old Testament. It appears only here in Kings.

The incident related in this passage is somewhat shocking to our modern, Western sense of morality, but we need to remember that in Old Testament times polygamous marriage and concubinage were legal and socially respectable. The king's extreme physical weakness, so dramatically highlighted by the necessity for taking the measure here described, precipitated the scramble for power with which the rest of the chapter is concerned. Abishag is to play an additional part in the story (2:17). A "Shunammite" is an inhabitant of Shunem near the Plain of Esdraelon.

Adonijah's Bid for the Throne (1:5-10)

The rest of this section illustrates the corrupting effect of polygamy on the life of the court. The kind of harem intrigues pictured here are typical of oriental monarchies down almost to the present day. Every one of the older sons hoped for the succession, and their mothers, each with her own coterie of advisers, naturally conspired on their sons' behalf. Adonijah, the fourth of the sons of David (II Sam. 3:4), would seem, after the deaths of Amnon and Absalom, to have had the best claim to the throne, but unwisely he showed his hand too soon. Among his partisans were two of the highest secular and religious officials of the state: Joab, the chief of the army, and Abiathar, one of the two chief priests. When Adonijah held a great banquet to celebrate his accession to the throne, he pointedly failed to invite his half brother Solomon and the men of Solomon's party. En-rogel, the scene of

the celebration, was a spring in the Kidron Valley not far outside
the city.

Solomon Becomes King (1:11-40)

If Adonijah had on his side two important officials, Solomon,
the son of Bathsheba, had two others: Benaiah, another high
officer in the army, and Zadok, the second of the two chief
priests. In addition, he was supported by the prophet Nathan,
who already had a close relationship to Bathsheba through his
intervention with the king on the occasion of her unhappy introduction to the court (II Sam. 12:1-15). Upon hearing of Adonijah's premature celebration of his rise to power, Nathan immediately reported the matter to Bathsheba, who promptly brought
news of it to the ailing king and reminded him of an alleged
promise to secure the throne for her own son. Her report to
David was seconded by Nathan, with the result that David made
arrangements to have Solomon anointed king without delay. The
ceremony took place at Gihon, another spring in the Kidron
Valley, not far from En-rogel. There Zadok and Nathan joined in
performing the sacred rite which conferred on Solomon the
character and authority of kingship. The Cherethites and Pele-
thites who assisted at the ceremony (vs. 38) were foreign mercenaries in the service of the king, under the direct control of
Benaiah (II Sam. 8:18). The mule on which Solomon rode was
the proper beast of royalty. The common people used asses,
while horses were not yet common or used as riding animals.

Adonijah's Discomfiture (1:41-53)

The two springs were out of sight of each other, though not
too far apart for hearing. When Joab, at Adonijah's feast, heard
the sound of the ceremonial trumpet, he knew that some event
of great importance was taking place and was soon informed
what it was. All the guests realized the implications and precipitately deserted the cause of Adonijah. Adonijah had good reason
to fear for his own life, since it had always been customary in the
Orient for kings, on their accession, to eliminate possible rivals
to the throne and Adonijah had put himself in especial danger by
his rash and presumptuous attempt to assert his claim. So he
immediately fled to the sanctuary and caught hold of the "horns"
of the altar, the projections at the four corners which were its
most sacred part. The sanctuary, of course, was not the Temple,

which was not yet built, but the sacred tent which David had erected to contain the Ark (II Sam. 6:17). Solomon gave him a pledge of safety, although, as we shall see in the next chapter, he took advantage of the first opportunity to void it. As a result of Solomon's pledge, Adonijah himself pledged formal allegiance to the new king.

Whether Adonijah or Solomon would have made the better king is a question no one can answer for certain. Although the principle of the succession of the eldest son had not yet been clearly established, Adonijah would seem, at first glance, to have had the better claim. It is interesting to note that he is described as a handsome man (vs. 6), like Absalom (II Sam. 14:25) and like David, their father (I Sam. 16:12). But, important as this may have seemed to the ancient Hebrews, who regarded physical beauty as a sign of divine favor, it is less impressive to us than the fact that he was evidently a spoiled child (vs. 6), like Absalom before him. Solomon, with all his faults, which were many, seems to have been a man of more civilized spirit and greater self-control.

David's Death and Solomon's Consolidation of Power (2:1-46)

David's Last Commands (2:1-12)

As we know all too well from the narrative in Second Samuel, David's character had its darker side, but up to the time of his death he had at least distinguished himself from his contemporaries by a consistent refusal to take revenge for injuries done to him (I Sam. 24:17; 25:33). We should be happier if we did not have to read how he blackened this record upon his deathbed, from which he ordered his son to take vengeance upon Joab, one of his most loyal supporters, and upon his enemy Shimei, whom he had previously forgiven (II Sam. 19:23). One must, however, take into account the ancient superstitions, which David shared, about bloodguilt and the power of a curse. Joab had undoubtedly shed much blood, though usually to the king's advantage (II Sam. 3:27; 18:14; 20:10), and in so far as the blood was innocent it still clung to David and his descendants after him, for it had been shed while Joab was in his service. Shimei had once cursed David (II Sam. 16:7-8), and the power of that curse was still alive. In the mysterious hour of death the power of superstition is probably at its strongest, so perhaps it is not surprising that David succumbed to its influence and left behind him these two dreadful orders. Their grimness is slightly alleviated by his affectionate remembrance of the kindness of Barzillai (vs. 7; see II Sam. 19:32).

David was buried in the royal city, Jerusalem, which he had captured and which had been renamed in his honor (vs. 10; see II Sam. 5:7).

Solomon's First Acts as King (2:13-46)

After David's death, Solomon succeeded in effectively eliminating his own personal enemies as well as those whom his father had doomed in his dying charge. In each case, there was at least the color of an excuse, but in the whole proceedings there is clear evidence of Solomon's determination that no trace of opposition should remain to threaten the internal peace and security of his realm. The establishment of the kingdom had introduced into Israel worldly customs and ways of thinking which were native to the other monarchies of the ancient Near East but foreign to the true genius of Israel. These events at the beginning of Solomon's reign show, quite as clearly as anything which was to come after, that Solomon was determined to become a king of the usual oriental type. Much of the later history recorded in the Books of Kings is the story of the struggle of the older ideals of Israel to reassert themselves against the alien ways which were beginning in this way to corrupt the purity and simplicity of ancient Israelite society. The great prophets were leaders in this struggle and never became quite reconciled to the idea of kingship in Israel.

The first victim, naturally enough, was Adonijah himself. He was foolish enough to ask that Abishag, David's concubine, be given to him as a kind of consolation prize. Either he was incredibly simple or else he really had some deeper design, for he must have known that to claim a king's concubine was equivalent to claiming the throne itself. This is illustrated by the conduct of Absalom when, after driving his father out of Jerusalem, he made his first act that of taking public possession of the royal harem (II Sam. 16:22). Even the intervention of Bathsheba was not enough to save Adonijah from the consequences of his folly, and he was summarily executed by the commander of the royal guard.

The second person to be punished for his part in assisting Adonijah was the priest Abiathar, one of David's oldest and most trusted friends, a companion since the days of his exile (I Sam. 22:20-23). After David's rise to the throne, Abiathar had been his chief priest until, following the conquest of Jerusalem, the mysterious Zadok had been appointed his associate, probably for reasons of policy (II Sam. 8:17). Zadok had been astute enough during the struggle for the throne to associate himself with the rising fortunes of Solomon, but Abiathar had evidently taken it for granted that Adonijah, as the eldest surviving son, would have the better chance. Now he must pay the price of his error. Both because of Abiathar's sacred character as a priest and because of his well-known loyalty to David, Solomon did not dare to treat him in as summary fashion as Adonijah and was content to banish him to the little country village of Anathoth, a short distance north of Jerusalem. The historian notes (vs. 27) that this could be taken as fulfilling the prophecy recorded in I Samuel 2:27-36. The prophet Jeremiah, who some three centuries later appeared among the priests of Anathoth, may well have been one of the descendants of Abiathar (Jer. 1:1).

When Joab heard of the fate of Adonijah and his chief supporter in the priesthood, he knew that his turn would certainly be next, and so he fled to the sanctuary for refuge. Solomon felt no need for restraint in dealing with him, since Joab's reputation for ruthlessness had already sufficiently alienated public sympathy. After a brief colloquy had failed to dislodge Joab from the sacred tent, Solomon ordered his henchman, Benaiah, to disregard his claim to right of sanctuary and kill him at the altar. The superstitious fears which helped to motivate the king in acting so precipitately are clearly underlined in verse 33. While the character of Joab was such as to forbid our feeling any particular regret at his end, it should in all fairness be recalled that his loyalty to David (who was his cousin) was beyond all question. He was the one chiefly responsible for David's victories both in foreign wars and in domestic insurrections. With the disposition of Abiathar and Joab, the way was now clear for advancing Solomon's partisans, Zadok and Benaiah, to the chief positions in church and army.

Greater sympathy perhaps is due to Shimei, a loyal adherent of the house of Saul, whose one crime had been to curse David on his expulsion from Jerusalem by Absalom and to assert that the king was getting exactly what he deserved. Solomon, probably foreseeing the course of events, promised to save his life as long as he stayed in Jerusalem. When, three years later, Shimei apparently either forgot the agreement or else unwisely presumed on the king's indulgence and went off on a legitimate business errand to the Philistine country, he gave Solomon the excuse for which he was looking and lost his life in consequence.

With all potential rivals eliminated, Solomon was now firmly established on the throne. Enemies would again arise, but at least they would be the result of honest opposition to Solomon's policies rather than of mere disappointment at his successful bid for power.

THE REIGN OF SOLOMON

I Kings 3:1—11:43

Preamble (3:1-28)

General Estimate of Solomon's Reign (3:1-3)

One must read the story of Solomon on several different levels. There is, first of all, the level of the final editors of the Books of Kings who, in an age of disaster and national disgrace, looked back with admiration to Solomon as the builder of the Temple, and to the age of Solomon as a time of peace and imperial grandeur—clear tokens, it would seem, of God's favor toward him. All the later history of Israel, with only a few bright interludes, appeared as a gradual decline into impotence and defeat. It seemed to the historians that such a king, in spite of some evidence to the contrary, must have been a good man, loyal to the Law of God and wise with God's wisdom above all later kings. This is the estimate which is given in verse 3 of the third chapter. Then, on the second level, there is the view of some of Solomon's contemporaries, who had a less profoundly religious point of view and were dazzled by the amazing material prosperity of his reign. Only a generation or so before, the Hebrews had been an impoverished, half-civilized group of tribes dominated by the "uncircumcised Philistines." Now they were a great power with subject states of their own and a capital city, adorned with magnificent buildings, which could bear comparison with the other capitals of the world. Although it was David who had laid the solid foundations of the new empire, it was unquestionably under Solomon that it attained its greatest heights of wealth and external magnificence. Such a king must obviously be a man of the greatest wisdom (that is, shrewdness or cleverness) in the worldly sense of the term. This is the estimate that is given in such passages as 4:20-34 and 10:1-8. Finally, there is the level of the modern scientific student of history, who is neither filled with the nostalgia of the Deuteronomic historians nor dazzled as were Solomon's contemporaries by the splendor of his court. The scientific historian must try to see Solomon as he really was, with his weaknesses as well as his obvious assets. This final estimate of Solomon is likely to be a good deal less favorable than that of his admiring contemporaries or of the Deuteronomic editors of Kings, although it will necessarily be based on evidence which comes from both these sources.

As the reader peruses the evidence, seeking to arrive at his own estimate, he should keep in mind at least the following facts: First, Solomon did not build his empire; he merely enjoyed the fruits of what David had already achieved. Second, the splendid monuments which he erected were not intended to serve the needs of his people but to enhance his own glory (even the Temple was primarily a private chapel). Third, his enormous income was only in part derived from the tribute of conquered states or from legitimate business enterprise; a large part of it was sucked from his subjects by forced labor and oppressive taxation. Fourth, while he was undoubtedly a sincere worshiper of Yahweh, the God of Israel, he saw nothing inconsistent in permitting—even in the precincts of the Temple—the worship of the gods of other nations. Finally, it must not be forgotten that the empire which he had inherited in such excellent condition had already begun to collapse before his death and the nation itself split into two violently antagonistic parts immediately upon the accession of his son. These items must be kept in mind when evaluating the two idealizing stories about Solomon which occupy most of the present chapter.

The chapter opens with a brief statement about Solomon's marriage to Pharaoh's daughter. This was only the first of a series of marriages to foreign princesses designed to cement the ties between Solomon's kingdom and other important surrounding nations. Verses 2 and 3 give the Deuteronomic historians' estimate of Solomon; notice that they must qualify even their approval

with the observation that the king continued to permit his people
to worship on the "high places," the hilltop sanctuaries where
Yahweh was worshiped as though he were merely one of the
ancient gods of Canaan. The elimination of these high places
would be one of the major goals of the Deuteronomic reform (II
Kings 23:8).

Two Stories About Solomon's Wisdom (3:4-28)

Both the stories told in the remainder of this chapter obviously
come from circles in which the character of Solomon was ideal-
ized. In the first (vss. 4-15) it is related that Solomon, presumably near the beginning of his reign, visited the great sanctuary
at Gibeon (the modern village of El Jib, a few miles northwest
of Jerusalem) to offer sacrifice. There God appeared to him in
a dream and asked him to select a gift with which he might bless
him. Solomon is reported to have chosen the gift of an understanding heart to enable him rightly to govern his people. As a
reward for his wise choice, he was given also the promise of
riches and honor. While there can be no doubt that, within his
limitations, Solomon was an intelligent man, the story really
reveals more about the people who told it than about Solomon.
Just as the story of George Washington and the cherry tree
shows the high value placed upon truth and honesty in early
American life, this story makes it clear that the men of the Old
Testament attached a far higher degree of value to intelligence
and understanding than to mere material success.

The second story (vss. 16-28) illustrates the kind of "wisdom"
which the Hebrews believed a ruler or judge should have, namely,
the shrewd insight which makes a man able to distinguish a true
witness from a false one and to bring the essential facts to light.
There is every reason to believe that Solomon did possess this
kind of naturally quick intelligence, however much he may have
been lacking in some of the higher forms of wisdom.

Solomon, Organizer of the Kingdom (4:1-28)

Since the age of Solomon was pre-eminently a time of peace,
there was little in the way of ordinary historical events to be
recorded. So, instead of dealing with his reign in the usual chronological fashion, the ancient historians preferred simply to relate
his achievements and the impression he made on his contem-

poraries. The heads under which they discuss him are, to use modern language: the Organizer, the Patron of Culture, the Builder, and the Merchant Prince. It would be well for the reader to keep these headings in mind as he reads the following chapters, for the same subjects sometimes recur in different passages. In all of these fields, Solomon was obviously a man of ability and deserves some of the praise he received, though it must not be forgotten that there was also a less praiseworthy side to each of them.

The first subject discussed is the way in which he organized the kingdom to bring it to maximum efficiency. David, who had created the empire, had also made considerable progress in this direction, but the main achievement was undoubtedly Solomon's.

The Cabinet (4:1-6)

We read first of all about the composition of the royal cabinet, the "high officials" (vs. 2). There is some confusion in this section, especially as concerns the priests, but the main points are clear and the confusion can be partly resolved by reference to other passages. With the growth of state organization it was important to have officials in charge of the public records. These were the "secretaries" and the "recorder" of verse 3. The latter word means properly "remembrancer" and probably refers to an official whose duty was to remind the king of projects which still needed to be accomplished. Benaiah was secretary of war as well as general of the army; Zadok was chief priest (the mention of Abiathar is certainly erroneous; see above, 2:26-27); the title "king's friend" applied to Zabud was an official designation and perhaps almost equivalent to "prime minister." A sinister note is struck by the designation of Adoniram as "in charge of the forced labor." One of the great weaknesses of Solomon's administration was his insistence upon wringing the last possible amount of money and other help from his subjects. This policy would bring about the disruption of the kingdom on Solomon's death and Adoniram (Adoram) was to play a most unhappy role on that occasion (12:18).

The Twelve Administrative Districts (4:7-19)

This section tells how Solomon reorganized the country so as to bring in a maximum income for the royal treasury. There are a number of historical puzzles in this list, but there seems to be

little doubt that it largely ignores the old boundaries of the separate tribes. This was no doubt partly for the sake of efficiency
but was also motivated by Solomon's desire to break down tribal
loyalties in the interest of creating a unified national state. It is
striking that Judah is not included on the list, possibly because
it was Solomon's own tribe and was therefore on the receiving
end of the arrangements. If Judah was, indeed, excluded from
having to pay its fair share of these impositions, this would provide another reason for the discontent with Solomon's rule which
was later manifested by the northern tribes.

The Splendor of Solomon's Reign (4:20-28)

The rest of the chapter is rather a rhapsodic celebration of
Solomon's success than a sober account of his accomplishments.
We are told in glowing language of the peace and prosperity of
the realm and of the great size of the empire over which Solomon
ruled. It extended from the Euphrates River on the north and
east to the borders of Egypt in the south. This, of course, was
ideally the territory which David had conquered and bequeathed
to his son. The ancient writer goes on to tell of the magnificence
of Solomon's court, certainly an example of "conspicuous consumption" on a very large scale. The whole system of administration which has been previously described had for its chief
object the regular maintenance of this luxurious manner of life.
What our author does not tell us is the cost of this splendor in
terms of life for the ordinary man. It is true that he makes some
general statements about the way in which all the nation partici-
pated in the peaceful and prosperous conditions of the time, but
these idyllic generalizations must certainly be qualified in view
of the rebellion which had already begun in Solomon's reign and
which was to break out in flaming revolt on his death (see also
the comment on chapter 11).

Solomon, the Patron of Culture (4:29-34)

Solomon's later reputation for wisdom is partly based upon a
certain ambiguity in the ancient Hebrew use of the word. "Wisdom" in the Old Testament *can* mean what we mean when we
use the term, but, especially in early passages, it can have other
meanings as well, all of which ultimately go back to the idea of
"skill." A "wise" man was originally a "skillful" man or a man of

"ability and intelligence" (see, for example, Exod. 31:1-6). Since skill can be manifested not only in the manual crafts but also in poetry, music, and other refined accomplishments of civilized society, "wisdom" could also mean a mastery of the arts of culture. It is probably in this sense that Solomon had his clearest title to "wisdom." It was Solomon who introduced his people to the culture of the ancient Near East. His court became a center where the amenities of civilized life were cultivated and the king himself showed considerable ability in these pursuits. The present passage speaks of his skill in composing "proverbs" and "songs" and his interest in natural history. Since this interest in culture, science, art, and philosophy was a new thing in Israel, Solomon is rightly remembered as the one who began it. The Wisdom Literature of the Old Testament (Proverbs, Ecclesiastes, Job) is a later product of the same movement, and it was inevitable that some of these books would be attributed to Solomon, as were even later books, such as The Wisdom of Solomon (in the Apocrypha) and the "Odes" of Solomon.

Solomon, the Builder (5:1—9:25)

King Solomon is best known as the builder of the Temple. It should be remembered, however, that the building of the Temple was not an independent enterprise, but was part of a great building program designed to make Jerusalem a worthy capital for so mighty a king. Solomon arranged for the construction of a large complex of palace buildings, and in that complex a temple for the God of Israel had its necessary place. This was in accord with the general practice of the other kings in the ancient Orient, whom Solomon was eager to emulate, but was not exactly in accord with the older traditions of the people of Israel. Even though there seems to have been some kind of permanent temple at Shiloh in the days of the Judges, the common tradition represented Yahweh as the God of a simple, nomadic people—a God who *preferred* to dwell in a movable shrine. He had accompanied the ancestors of Israel in a tent ("the tabernacle") during their desert wanderings. Even David had been satisfied with erecting a tent to house the sacred Ark when he brought it to Jerusalem. But Solomon was resolved that his palace should not be that of an uncultured, still spiritually nomadic, people. It should be like the palaces of other great kings and, if that was to be so, it must necessarily include a magnificent temple, a splendid royal chapel, beautified by all the resources that human effort could muster.

Preliminary Arrangements (5:1-18)

One of the difficulties in carrying out Solomon's scheme was that his people, having but just emerged into the "civilized" world, had no artisans who were capable of designing or building such structures as Solomon had in mind. They could provide the crude, unskilled labor, but the master workmen and most of the materials had to come from elsewhere. The obvious source for both the skill and the fine wood needed was in the neighboring country of Phoenicia (the present-day Lebanon). Here there were great cedar forests and a long tradition of artistic achievement. So Solomon's first step was to enter into a treaty with Hiram, the friendly Phoenician monarch, to obtain the necessary cedar wood and also Lebanese workmen who could supervise cutting and preparing it. The wood was to be floated in large rafts along the seacoast from Lebanon to Palestine. This was, of course, a commercial arrangement, and verse 11 tells the price which Solomon agreed to pay. The amount was so enormous (220,000 bushels of wheat and 180,000 gallons of oil) that we are not surprised to find out later that Solomon apparently went bankrupt and had to cede part of his territory to settle the debt (9:11).

In addition to these vast sums to be paid in kind, Solomon also had to arrange for ordinary labor to be done. We now see the full significance of the presence of a "secretary for forced labor" in the royal cabinet. Adoniram was in charge of the entire project (vs. 14), with the responsibility of keeping ten thousand men constantly at work in the Lebanese mountains. This large corps of laborers was allowed two months at home for every month spent in Phoenicia. This amounted to a 33 and 1/3 per cent tax on the time and earning capacity of the men involved. One can easily imagine the bitter feelings aroused by a measure so oppressive and so contrary to the older traditions of Israel.

We also learn from this paragraph that stone, as well as wood, was obtained from Lebanon and that, once again, the skilled work was necessarily done by the Phoenicians. Particular mention is made of the Gebalites, the inhabitants of the important port of Gebal (later Byblos) some distance north of the capital city of Tyre.

The Construction of the Temple (6:1-38)

In order to understand the design of Solomon's Temple, one must realize that a temple in the ancient world was not a church but a dwelling place for a god. The king lived in a palace, magnificently adorned as a proper setting for his dignity as a ruler among the rulers of the earth; his god must also have a palace, suitable to *his* dignity as a ruler among the rulers of heaven. In Hebrew there is one word which means temple and palace (it is translated "palace" in 21:1). There was no room for worshipers within a temple, any more than there was room in the royal palace for large groups of ordinary citizens. Only the king's servitors would be admitted within the palace and only the special ministers of the god would have access to the temple. If the people wished to show their devotion to their earthly king, they would have to gather *outside* his palace and shout their acclamations; so the worshipers of the god would assemble in the courtyard of the temple to offer their gifts and sing his praises.

Obviously, these ideas are not basically Hebrew or biblical, but we have already noted that Solomon was deliberately introducing customs which were not those of his own people in order to accommodate the life of Israel to the life of other "cultured" peoples of the ancient Near East. The whole idea of a temple for the God of Israel was offensive to certain conservative groups and would always remain so (see, for example, Isa. 66:1). Even the present narrative shows traces of this tension (8:27). In the New Testament, Stephen represents the conservative point of view in its most extreme form. At the trial before his martyrdom, he concluded a survey of Israel's history with a contemptuous reference to Solomon's building of the Temple which makes it evident that for him this was Israel's culminating act of apostasy (Acts 7:44-50).

The date of the beginning of the Temple is said to have been the fourth year of Solomon's reign. According to the best calculation, this would be 962 B.C. If the date of 480 years after the Exodus from Egypt could be taken literally, we should be able to date that basic event in Israel's history with absolute certainty, but unfortunately it seems to be inconsistent with information provided elsewhere in the Bible and with what we know from archaeology and secular history.

The fact that the Temple was the palace of God rather than a place of worship explains its surprisingly small dimensions as given in verse 2. It was 90 feet long, 30 feet wide, and 45 feet high, a "cubit" being approximately 18 inches. The description in the remainder of the chapter is somewhat fragmentary and is not always easy to follow, even with careful reading. The Temple was, however, a relatively simple structure, quite similar in form to other ancient Near Eastern temples which are still standing or which have been uncovered by archaeologists. Since the Hebrews had no tradition of temple building themselves, Solomon had no choice but to follow a design which was already common in that part of the world. The master workmen came from Phoenicia, so it may be assumed that the basic plan was Phoenician.

We learn first of all about the exterior of the building. At the front there was a small vestibule, and round about, built up against the walls on three sides, were three stories of small chambers, possibly for storing various appurtenances of worship. Above these was a row of windows which illuminated the "nave" (the Holy Place), but (as we learn later) not the "inner sanctuary" (the *Most* Holy Place). Verse 7 notes that the stone was prepared at the quarry, not on the Temple grounds, no doubt for religious reasons.

Verses 11-13 seem to come from the Deuteronomic historians who finally edited the Books of Kings. They wish to emphasize that God will not dwell among his people simply because a magnificent palace has been built for him. Not even the king can bribe God in this way. God's presence is always conditional, depending upon the moral attitudes of the people who worship him. The Temple has value only when men obey the ordinances and commandments of God and "walk in them." It was along these lines that the great prophets spoke, and it was only by insisting upon this qualification that the basic religious tradition of Israel was able to adjust itself to the existence of the Temple at all.

For understanding the interior arrangement of the Temple, we have to study not only this account but also the description of the "tabernacle" in Exodus 25-31, 36-40, which had approximately the same plan. Some information is also obtained from the description of the *future* Temple in Ezekiel 40-43. The Temple proper, beyond the vestibule, was divided into two rooms of unequal size. The "nave," sometimes called the "holy place," was the first and larger of the two. This was the room in which the priests regularly performed certain functions throughout the year. Beyond the "holy place" was the "most holy place" ("the holy of holies" or "inner sanctuary"). This room was in the shape of a cube 30 feet in length, breadth, and height (vs. 20). As we have noted, this room was not provided with windows and so was perfectly dark, a suitable place for the God of Israel to dwell (compare 8:12). In these interior rooms, no stone was to be seen. The floors were covered with cypress wood and the walls and ceilings were of carved cedar. In addition, it is all said to have been covered with gold.

In any other temple of the ancient Orient, the inner sanctuary would have been occupied by the statue of the god, it being his own private chamber. But since images of Yahweh were forbidden by Hebrew tradition, this was impossible in Israel. This was a law which even Solomon would not have dared to break. However, the room was not entirely vacant, for certain symbols of God's presence were there, notably the Ark (8:6) and the "cherubim." The cherubim were other-worldly beings, part beast and part bird, such as are also to be found connected with the temples of the gods in other ancient lands. In Hebrew poetic thought, they accompanied Yahweh wherever he went and their outstretched wings formed the base of his throne (compare Ps. 18:10). Yahweh is sometimes referred to as the one "who is enthroned on the cherubim" (I Sam. 4:4). So it was natural that in his private chamber in the Temple there should be images of these creatures. They were carved of olive wood and were so arranged that their wings spread across the whole width of the room, touching the walls on both sides, with the inner wing of each touching the wing of the other in the middle. These images also are said to have been overlaid with gold. Other smaller figures of cherubim, together with flowers and palm trees, formed the pattern in which the walls of the rooms were carved.

Between the "nave" and the inner sanctuary there were carved wooden doors. The comparable opening in the Tabernacle in the desert is said to have been covered by a curtain (Exod. 26:33), and, according to II Chronicles 3:14, the Temple of Solomon had such a curtain also. There was certainly one in the Temple of Herod, since the Gospels relate that it was torn at the time of the crucifixion (Mark 15:38).

This door or curtain separating the "nave" from the inner sanctuary occupies a crucial point in the thinking of the New

Testament writer of the Letter to the Hebrews (although his argument is based on the arrangement of the Tabernacle rather than the Temple). In old Israel, only the high priest, once in the year on the Day of Atonement, was allowed to pass through into the direct presence of God. But Christ, the great High Priest of the New Age, has, through his death and resurrection, passed through this door "once for all" (Heb. 9:12) and opened the way for all men to come boldly into the divine Presence (Heb. 10:19-22).

The Construction of the Palace (7:1-12)

It is a little startling to note at the end of chapter 6 that Solomon spent seven years in building the house of God, while at the beginning of chapter 7 it is said that he spent thirteen years building a house for himself! Yet one must not judge him too harshly, for the construction of a great complex of royal buildings was his main objective and the Temple was only one part of the project. There can be little doubt that Solomon did all in his power to make the Temple worthy of the whole ensemble.

His palace was, of course, far more complicated than the Temple. It was a whole group of buildings, including among other things, an armory, rooms for the administration of government, and private quarters for the king, his harem, and the members of his family. The armory bore the poetic name of "the House of the Forest of Lebanon," so called because of the three rows of cedar pillars which supported the roof (to confirm the use for which this structure was built, see 10:17 and Isa. 22:8). The "Hall of Pillars" in verse 6 may have been the external portico of the "House of the Forest." The description of these buildings begins with the one farthest from the Temple (to the south) and then moves on to those which were closer. The next was the throne room, where the king held public audience. Last, and closest to the Temple, were the private quarters of the king and his family, with a special palace set apart for his Egyptian wife.

The Furnishing of the Temple (7:13-51)

The almost exclusively religious interest of the authors responsible for this history is clearly shown by the brief space they allot to the secular buildings, important as these must have been in Solomon's scheme, and their haste to get back to the story of the Temple. Having described the *building* of the Temple, they now go on to give an account of the various articles which were prepared for its furnishing. The artisan of the bronze furniture for the courtyard was a certain Hiram of Tyre (not the king of that name previously mentioned; Hiram was a common Phoenician name), who was of Hebrew descent through his mother but a Phoenician by citizenship and training. The reader will note the use of the term "wisdom" in connection with him in its original sense of "skill."

The first objects mentioned are the two sacred bronze pillars, named Jachin and Boaz, which stood in front of the Temple. These pillars had no structural function, as they were entirely detached from the building, but were put there simply because such pillars were commonly found in other temples of the ancient East. They may ultimately have been connected with the "pillars" which were set up in Canaanite high places (Deut. 12:3). The names are possibly derived from the first words of Hebrew inscriptions which were written on them.

The second item is the "molten sea," an enormous bronze basin, presumably constructed to store the water used for ceremonial ablutions. It stood on the backs of twelve bronze bulls, facing outward in groups of three toward the four directions of the compass. The fact that these bull images were found in the Temple at Jerusalem, while Jeroboam is later condemned for having set up similar images in his sanctuaries at Dan and Bethel (12:28-29), reminds us that the history of Israel's religion was a good deal more complicated than a casual reading of the narratives would indicate. The struggle to preserve the ancient religion from contamination by paganism was a long one, which came to a definitive conclusion only with the Babylonian Exile. Since the great bowl was called a "sea," it is assumed that it originally must have had some mythological meaning; it may have been a symbol of the primeval sea which, according to ancient ideas, had to be conquered and confined before order could be imposed on the universe (see, for example, Ps. 74:12-13; Job 38:8-11).

Apparently in order to convey water from the "sea" to the point at which it was used, there were also ten small basins on wheels, colorfully decorated with lions, oxen, cherubim, and palm trees. Verse 39 tells where these various objects were placed in the Temple court. The "sea" would have stood just south of the altar of sacrifice, which faced the entrance to the Temple but curiously enough is not mentioned in this chapter (although it is

included in the Chronicler's parallel account in II Chronicles
4:1).

Verses 40-46 are a summary of Hiram's work, in which reference is also made to various minor appurtenances of worship such as pots and shovels. All these articles were cast in the clay soil of the Jordan Valley and then brought up to Jerusalem.

Finally (vss. 48-50), there is a summary account of the golden vessels which Solomon provided for the interior of the Temple building. The golden "altar" was not really an altar, but an incense stand, as we learn from the account in Exodus 30:1-10. The table of "the bread of the Presence" was for the regular offering of loaves to the Deity (Exod. 25:30). There were also ten lampstands. In the later Temples (of Zerubbabel and Herod) there was a single seven-branched lampstand, the form of which is familiar to us from its being pictured on the Arch of Titus at Rome. All these objects stood in the "nave" or "holy place," the large room between the vestibule and the inner sanctuary or "most holy place."

The Dedication of the Temple (8:1-66)

While there is undoubtedly a core of historic fact in this chapter, it seems clear that the account is not for the most part taken from ancient contemporary documents, but is rather a free composition of the final (Deuteronomic) editors of the Books of Kings. This is particularly true of the long and, in some respects, very beautiful dedicatory prayer which is placed upon the lips of Solomon and which occupies most of the chapter. It was a common practice among ancient historians to write appropriate speeches for their characters on great occasions. The speeches found in the work of the Greek historian Thucydides are classic examples of this custom.

The most important thing was to bring into the newly completed inner sanctuary of the Temple the Ark, the most sacred symbol of the presence of God, which, ever since David's early days, had been kept in the shelter of a tent in the old royal city, a short distance to the south. To mark this solemn occasion the king summoned all the leaders of the nation to a festival assembly in Jerusalem. The dedication ceremonies were delayed for eleven months (compare 6:38 with 8:2) so that they might coincide with the annual New Year celebration which occurred in the seventh month (Tishri; or Ethanim, as it was called in Solomon's time). This was the most sacred season of the year, still commemorated by the Jews with the celebration of Rosh Hashana, the Day of Atonement, and the Feast of Tabernacles. While no description of the procession accompanying the Ark is given here, the details can easily be imagined by reading the vivid account in II Samuel 6:1-19 of David's original bringing of the Ark into the capital city.

The contents of the Ark have always been a subject for speculation. It may originally have been only an empty box in which, or on which, the Deity was supposed to dwell. The Deuteronomists, with their strongly moral conception of religion, were sure that it contained the tablets of the Law of God. This is the view which is represented here. Whatever was in it, the importance of the Ark lay in the fact that it represented in a concrete way the actual Presence of God. This close association of God and the Ark is strikingly illustrated in Numbers 10:35-36, where an ancient song seems to address the Ark as though it were God himself, and in I Samuel 4:5-7, where the Philistines, on hearing that the Ark has arrived in the Hebrew camp, cry out fearfully that "God" (rather than "the gods") had come into the camp. When the Ark was finally placed under the protecting wings of the cherubim, the Temple, we are told, was filled with "the glory" of God, the luminescent cloud which was believed to mark his Presence.

The brief, poetic utterance which follows (vs. 12) is no doubt an authentic composition of Solomon's. The first line in the Revised Standard Version is not found in the Hebrew, but is preserved in the Greek translation of the Old Testament (the Septuagint), which also relates the important fact that the poem had been preserved in "the Book of Song" (or "of Jashar," an old collection of Hebrew poetry mentioned elsewhere in Joshua 10:13 and II Samuel 1:18). There is a basic contradiction between the theology of Solomon, who really believed that he could build for God "an exalted house, a place for thee to dwell in for ever," and that of the later Deuteronomic editors who, in the course of the long dedicatory prayer which they place upon his lips, have him say, "But will God indeed dwell on the earth? Behold, heaven and the highest heaven cannot contain thee; how much less this house which I have built!" (vs. 27). For the Deuteronomists, it was not God himself in the fullness of his Being who dwelt in the Temple, but only his "name" (vs. 29). This was an attempt on

their part to reconcile their belief in the universal presence of an
all-powerful and all-knowing God with the conviction that in
some sense the divine Presence was to be found uniquely in the
Temple. King Solomon, who belonged to a much simpler and
more naïve age, had no such intellectual difficulties.

After pronouncing the dedicatory sentence, the king turns and
delivers a brief address to the people (vss. 14-21) in which he
attempts to explain the paradox that David, the king especially
favored by God, had never built a Temple for him. Other passages of Scripture wrestle with this difficulty: one says that the
God of Israel did not care to dwell in temples (II Sam. 7:5-6);
another, that David was forbidden to build one because he was
a man of blood (I Chron. 22:8). Such discrepancies cast no reflection on the historical value and spiritual authority of Scripture. They arise from the fact that the people of Israel, like ourselves, were interested in the question of human motives and
gave different answers to problems of this kind which objective
history so often must leave unsolved. How difficult it is even
today to discover just why a person has acted or failed to act in
a certain way! If we still insist on trying to find a solution to the
mystery of David's conduct in this matter, the best answer is
probably the first one given above, namely, that he did not build
a temple because it did not seem to him that the God of Israel
either needed or wanted one.

The long dedication prayer (vss. 22-53) requires little comment, though it is worthy of a careful reading. It begins with an
account of God's dealings with the family of David (vss. 23-26),
continues with a prayer that, even though God cannot really
dwell in a temple, he would hear his people when they come
there to present their petitions (vss. 27-30). It then specifies at
length the various occasions on which prayer was likely to be
made: in a criminal trial, where everything hangs upon the truth
or falsity of a man's oath (vss. 31-32); after defeat in war (vss.
33-34); in time of drought (vss. 35-36) or famine and pestilence
(vss. 37-40); there would be prayers made by foreigners (vss.
41-43); prayers before a battle (vss. 44-45); and prayers in time
of exile (vss. 46-53). This prayer is followed by another of more
general character (vss. 56-61), which ends with a characteristic
exhortation to moral obedience (vs. 61). The chapter then concludes with an account of the enormous sacrifices which were
offered upon this occasion. The bronze altar of sacrifice, which

stood before the Temple (strangely passed over in the enumeration of the furnishings in chapter 7) is here mentioned for the first time (vs. 64). The "burnt offering" was a sacrifice wholly consumed on the altar (Lev. 1:3-17); the "cereal offering" was an offering of grain (Lev. 2); while "peace offerings" were actual religious banquets or communion feasts in which only a small portion of the sacrificial animal (especially the fat parts) was offered on the altar (Lev. 3). The dedication festival lasted seven days. "The entrance of Hamath" (vs. 65) is in the valley between Mount Hermon and the Lebanon Mountains; "the Brook of Egypt" is the small stream which marks the southern border of Palestine.

The Temple's Destruction Foreshadowed (9:1-9)

We have already noted the custom of ancient historians of formulating speeches for their characters. One value of this method of writing history is that it permits the historian to express his ideas and his interpretation of events without interrupting the course of the narrative. Since the final edition of the Books of Kings was published during the Babylonian Exile, when the Temple of Solomon and all the city around it had been reduced to ruins, we should naturally expect to find intimations of this fact even early in the story, together with some attempt to point the moral. The present passage justifies our expectations. It takes the form of a second oracle delivered to Solomon like the one given at the high place of Gibeon (3:4-15), the burden of which is that Solomon and his descendants would continue to rule in Israel only so long as they were loyal to God and obeyed his law (a basic theme of the Deuteronomists). The positive aspect of this doctrine is stated in verses 1-5. The inevitable corollary, however, is found in verses 6-9. If king and people fail in loyalty to their God, they will be carried into captivity and the Temple of which they are so proud will be laid level with the ground. Those for whom these words were written knew that the catastrophe had taken place and drew from it the salutary lesson of verse 9. The disaster had befallen them, not because Yahweh the God of Israel was powerless to protect his people, but "Because they forsook the LORD their God who brought their fathers out of the land of Egypt, and laid hold on other gods, and worshiped them and served them." The Deuteronomists were not, of course, interested merely in evoking a mood of regret for past mistakes, but rather in arousing their people to genuine repentance and renewal. Their God was not simply a God of justice who punishes men for their misdeeds, but a God of grace who is eager to forgive sins and restore the sinner. Solomon's prayer of dedication also contains a passage which is obviously directed toward the people in exile in Babylon and which states the conditions under which they may hope for better things to come (8:46-53).

Territory Ceded to the Phoenicians (9:10-14)

The tremendous sums of money which Solomon had to pay for his building program were too heavy a drain on the resources of his kingdom, so, in order to fulfill his obligations, he was compelled to sell Hiram a part of his territory in the north. The Chronicler found this procedure so obnoxious and incredible that he reverses it and represents Hiram ("Huram") as having ceded the land to Solomon! (II Chron. 8:2). The explanation of the name of the territory in verse 13 is a rather farfetched pun in Hebrew (Cabul is equivalent to "Like Nothing").

Solomon's Further Building Activities (9:15-25)

This section is somewhat confused, but the elements are easily disentangled. It speaks first of all of the use Solomon made of the principle of forced labor in order to obtain sufficient workers for his building schemes. Verses 20-22 state that only the descendants of the old Canaanite population were enslaved in this way, the Hebrews being given privileged status as warriors and supervisors (but see 5:13; 12:4). The rest of the section is chiefly concerned with Solomon's other building activities. The "Millo" may have been a fortress connected with the palace. Hazor was an important city in Galilee; Megiddo, an ancient stronghold in the Valley of Esdraelon (here was one of the chariot cities to be mentioned in 10:26). Gezer was an unconquered Canaanite city, west of Jerusalem on the edge of the coastal plain, which had been captured by the Egyptian king and given to his daughter as a dowry on the occasion of her marriage to Solomon. Beth-horon is northwest of Jerusalem on the western slope of the Judean mountains. Baalath has not been identified with certainty but was apparently southwest of Jerusalem, while Tamar was on the Egyptian border. All of these cities were of strategic importance and were rebuilt during Solomon's reign.

Solomon, the Merchant Prince (9:26—10:29)

Solomon's Fleet on the Red Sea (9:26-28)

The fourth important field of Solomon's activity was that of industry, trade, and commerce. This was one of the chief sources of his wealth. Since he controlled all the territory down to the Gulf of Aqabah, lines of communication were open to the fabulous lands of the farther East—South Arabia, Somaliland, even India—and Solomon exploited this fact to the best of his ability. At the head of the Gulf of Aqabah (the site of Ezion-geber and Eloth) he built a fleet of ships for the Eastern trade. Since the Hebrews were totally ignorant of the arts of sailing, he once again had to turn to Hiram of Tyre for technical assistance. The Phoenicians were the great seafaring nation of the ancient world, driven to maritime pursuits by their situation on a narrow coastal plain with the high Lebanon Mountains immediately at their back. So Solomon's ships and Hiram's sailors began to ply the waters of the Red Sea, their first voyages taking them at least as far as Ophir, which must lie somewhere in South Arabia, from which they brought back a cargo of gold said to have been worth about $10,000,000!

The Visit of the Queen of Sheba (10:1-13)

The mention of Ophir provides the editors with an opportunity to introduce the romantic story of the Queen of Sheba, whose domain was located in South Arabia. The subject of the story is ostensibly the "wisdom" of Solomon rather than his mercantile activities. We may be certain, however, that the visit of the queen was not simply for the purpose of beholding Solomon's glory and listening to his clever talk. Underneath the surface of polite convention and social converse, she undoubtedly had more serious motives—the establishment of good diplomatic relations and the increase of trade. The story is one which has caught the imagination of all readers and has been expanded into a more elaborate legend among the Arabs and the Ethiopians, the latter believing that their emperors were descended from a liaison which began on this occasion. Jesus used the Queen of Sheba's thirst for wisdom to castigate, by comparison, the men of his generation who would not listen to a greater wisdom than that of Solomon (Matt. 12:42). In the manner of ancient rulers, she came laden

with presents for her host, and when she had seen the incredible
luxury of his court and heard the deft answers he gave to her
questions, she was left breathless ("there was no more spirit in
her") and gave him gifts which were lavish even by oriental
standards. The legend of Solomon's wealth and "wisdom" rises to
its greatest climax in this story. But as the modern reader hears
the tale it has a false glitter, and he finds it easy to understand the
judgment of Jesus, who said that the flowers in the meadow display a greater and a truer glory than that of Solomon (Matt.
6:28-29).

More About Solomon's Commercial Ventures (10:14-29)

The story of the Queen of Sheba includes incidental mention
of several of the important items which were imported from
South Arabia: gold, spices, jewels, and "almug" trees (vss. 11-
12); the latter were rare and valuable trees which have as yet not
been satisfactorily identified. The enormous income which ac-
crued to Solomon's treasury from this trade is indicated by the
figures given in verse 14 for the importation of gold. While it is
not easy to translate ancient units of wealth into modern terms,
due to the tremendous differences in purchasing power, 666 tal-
ents of gold can be estimated roughly at $16,000,000. This may
be an exaggerated figure, but there can be no doubt that, even
when all allowances have been made, it was a princely sum.
Besides his direct profits from trade, Solomon was constantly
being enriched also by taxes paid by other traders and merchants
and by the tribute of his satraps and the kings of subject states.
The following verses describe two examples of the "conspicuous
consumption" which this income made possible. In the royal
armory, the "House of the Forest of Lebanon," there were 200
large decorative shields, of a type big enough to cover the whole
body, and 300 small round hand shields, all overlaid with gold.
They would not stay there long! (See 14:26.) There was also a
gold and ivory throne, decorated with twelve lions. Israel had
come a long way since the days of Saul's simple rule, when the
king held court at a small village, under a tamarisk tree (I Sam.
22:6). The obviously hyperbolical language of verses 21, 23-25
warns the reader against taking too literally everything that is
said about the grandeur of Solomon's reign. Verse 22 tells of
further imports by Solomon's merchant marine which brought
him not only ivory and precious metals, but exotic animals from

distant lands—"apes, and peacocks" (or, perhaps, as indicated in the margin, "baboons"; the meaning of the Hebrew word is uncertain). The "ships of Tarshish" were great vessels of a type capable of going to Tarshish, at the western end of the Mediterranean.

Another important aspect of Solomon's business enterprise, which has been correctly interpreted only in quite recent years, was his trade in horses, described in verses 26-29. The "chariot cities," which contained great stables, were intended to serve commercial as well as military purposes. A fine example of such a collection of stables, providing accommodation for 400 horses, has been uncovered in the excavation of Megiddo, the most important site in the Valley of Esdraelon (compare 9:15). Some interpreters think that "Kue" in verse 28 refers to Cilicia in southern Asia Minor; some also think that the word translated "Egypt" really refers to a different region, bordering on Cilicia. In any event, Solomon is here pictured as playing the role of a middleman, buying horses, which were of immense value for military purposes, from one region and selling them in another. Chariots, possibly purchased in Egypt, also played a part in these transactions.

The importance of archaeology has been demonstrated strikingly in recent years by the discovery at the site of Ezion-geber (see 9:26) of a blast furnace, ingeniously constructed to make use of the prevailing winds, which dates from Solomon's times. Here, it is evident, the king exploited the copper mines of the neighborhood and thus provided himself with an additional source of wealth. So, to the names of king, patron of culture, builder, and merchant, we must now add the title of "industrialist."

The Dark Side of Solomon's Reign (11:1-40)

It has been intimated several times before that Solomon's reign was not so entirely characterized by peace, prosperity, and wisdom as the superficial reader might imagine. In chapter 11 we are suddenly confronted with concrete evidence of the fact. The Deuteronomic historians, who wished on the whole to present a favorable picture of Solomon, were unwilling simply to pass over the evidence of his disloyalty to the traditions of Israel and his numerous errors of judgment, although the Chronicler had no hesitation in doing exactly this (compare the summary of Solomon's reign in II Chronicles 9:22-31). They have, however, collected the material in a single chapter which appears at the end of the story and which might, therefore, be interpreted as meaning that his folly was confined to his later years. But this is too simple an interpretation of the evidence. The weakness of Solomon's reign, which became blindingly clear in the events which immediately followed his death, was grounded in certain fundamental mistakes in policy—and in personal character—which were typical of his rule from beginning to end.

First of all, one notes his love of luxury and the emphasis on external display, which are so foreign to the Bible and to the temper of the ancient Hebrew people. The enormous harem which he attached to his court, described in the opening verses of this chapter, was a striking manifestation of this side of his character. That is not to say that Solomon was unduly given to sexual indulgence; there is no evidence that he was worse than other men of his time in this respect. The purpose of the harem was not so much to provide the ruler with opportunities for private debauchery as it was to show the wealth and magnificence of its owner. A man who could support 700 wives and 300 concubines was not a man whose resources could be measured by any ordinary human standards. To have so large a domestic establishment was perhaps equivalent in modern terms to owning a fleet of yachts! It is interesting to note that the collection of a great harem of this kind is specifically forbidden to the king in the later Deuteronomic law (Deut. 17:17).

But we also see from this passage that there was an even more basic weakness in Solomon's character: he had never grasped for himself the real meaning of Israel's distinctive religion. He was, of course, by his own lights, a faithful worshiper of Yahweh. But for him, as for many other ordinary Israelites, both in his time and later, Yahweh was not the sole God of heaven and earth, the majestic Creator of the cosmos and the Giver of the moral law, but merely the God of Israel—a national deity like the deities of other peoples. Both the old religion of Israel and the later religion of the Hebrew prophets claimed that the God of Israel was a "jealous" God who forbade his worshipers to have any other gods before him, but beside this high religion there was always a popular religion which was much more easygoing, which was tolerant of the age-old superstitions of the Canaanites and looked upon Yahweh as a tribal god just as the Moabites looked upon their god Chemosh or the Ammonites looked upon

Milcom. This popular religion was essentially Solomon's religion, except that in his case these tendencies were greatly reinforced by his policy of introducing among his somewhat backward, "uncivilized" people the common culture of the ancient Near East and remaking them according to the pattern of surrounding nations. He saw no harm in allowing his wives to worship their own gods in chapels which he built for them and in occasionally participating himself in such worship. His was an easygoing tolerance of all gods, and he no doubt regarded the adherents of Israel's older religious traditions as narrow-minded fanatics. The position which he represented is called "syncretism"—a tendency to make one's religion a mixture of many religions. Syncretism was the chief enemy against which the later prophets had to contend. They insisted that the old ways—that is, the old Hebrew ways—were the right ways (Jer. 6:16).

If Solomon's "wisdom" was not entirely wise, neither was the peace of his reign totally undisturbed. In verses 14-22, we read of a revolt in Edom, the kingdom southeast of the Dead Sea, which David had added to his empire (II Sam. 8:13-14) and which had great strategic importance since it controlled the routes of access to the Red Sea. Hadad, a prince of the Edomite royal line, had escaped to Egypt at the time of David's conquest, but on Solomon's accession to the throne he returned to his own country and there began to work for the independence of the Edomite kingdom and the re-establishment of his own authority. Notice that the general impression given by the narrative that such events occurred only toward the end of Solomon's reign is contradicted by the explicit statement that the trouble in Edom started at the very beginning (vs. 21). Another, and entirely successful, revolt took place in Syria, which David also had conquered and made a part of his empire (II Sam. 8:5-6). A certain commander in the Syrian army, by the name of Rezon, had revolted against both his old master, Hadadezer, and his new master, David. Living for a while as the captain of a group of renegades, he finally succeeded in capturing the city of Damascus, which he made his capital and where he continually made trouble for Solomon. He was the founder of the Syrian kingdom which was to continue in intermittent conflict with the kings of Israel through the centuries which followed and which came to an end only with the conquest of Damascus by the Assyrians (II Kings 16:9).

Finally, we hear of the most ominous disturbance of all: rumblings of revolt among the northern tribes of Israel itself (vss. 26-40). The hero of the revolt, of whom we shall hear more in the next chapter, was Jeroboam the son of Nebat, a young man of outstanding ability who had risen to the post of administrator of forced labor among the northern tribes ("the house of Joseph," vs. 28). Note that this verse contradicts the optimistic statement of 9:22. Evidently Jeroboam became increasingly resentful against the treatment accorded to his own people and committed some kind of insubordinate act, unspecified in the present version of the story, which put him outside the law and forced him to escape to Egypt. Eventually he returned to become the first king of the Northern Kingdom, Israel. It is significant that Jeroboam is said to have been prompted to his revolt by a prophet, Ahijah, from the ancient Hebrew shrine at Shiloh (vs. 29). Whatever may be the facts underlying this narrative, which is told in characteristically Deuteronomic style, the prophet is represented as playing a role typical of the later northern prophets, Elijah and Elisha. He was a defender of the ancient traditions which Solomon had violated, a defender of the underdog, who did not hesitate to use political means to attain his ends. Shishak (vs. 40), the king of Egypt at this time, is the first of the Pharaohs to be mentioned by name in the Bible. We shall meet him again in 14:25.

The Death of Solomon (11:41-43)

The long record of Solomon's reign concludes with a brief note concerning his death and a reference to the most important sourcebook from which the Deuteronomists drew their facts.

THE HISTORY OF THE DIVIDED KINGDOMS

I Kings 12:1—II Kings 17:41

The Revolt of Northern Israel (12:1-24)

The division between the Hebrews of the south (Judah) and those of the north (Israel) had very deep roots, going back to the days of the settlement in Canaan. One of the important historical questions which still perplex students of the Old Testa-

ment is that of the original relationship between these two groups.
Were they, as the Book of Joshua represents, two parts of a
single great people who invaded Palestine at the same time and
became separate only after the Conquest, or were they, as many
modern interpreters think, two originally quite separate groups,
related to each other only in a general way, who entered the
country at different periods, perhaps as much as two centuries
apart, and only later united into a single great Israelite confedera-
tion? Whatever may be the answer to this question, which is too
large to be entered into here, it is certain that the sense of sepa-
rateness was always a strong one. Until the time of David their
immediate contacts with each other were hampered by the fact
that a line of Canaanite cities, of which Jerusalem was the chief,
divided the territory of one from that of the other. While they
were united in government under Saul, it was not until David's
conquest of Jerusalem that they could live together as a unified
nation within continuous territorial boundaries. But even under
David's rule the old tensions were still manifest. He ruled over
Judah alone for seven years before he became king of Israel also
(II Sam. 5:1-5), and toward the end of his reign a serious revolt
broke out against him among the northern tribes under the
leadership of Sheba the son of Bichri, which was suppressed only
by the most severe countermeasures (II Sam. 20:1-22). So it is
not surprising that, under the far less popular and less effective
rule of Solomon, discontent should continue to grow and finally
eventuate, in the time of his son Rehoboam, in a complete rupture between the two parts of the nation—a rupture which was
never healed and would still be evident in New Testament times
in the antagonism between Jews and Samaritans.

That the nation was in essence a kind of dual monarchy, with
two capitals, is shown by the fact that Rehoboam, Solomon's
son, had to go to Shechem, the chief religious and political ral-
lying point of the northern tribes, to receive their allegiance after
his accession to the throne. They were not willing to bestow their
loyalty, however, until they received from him some pledge that
the oppressive measures instituted by Solomon would be relaxed.
Rehoboam, who evidently possessed neither his grandfather David's personal qualities of leadership nor his father's native shrewdness, appealed to his counselors for advice in the crisis, but was
so foolish as to reject the moderate counsel of the older men and
accept instead the recommendations of the young hotheads of his

entourage, who felt that any hint of a willingness to compromise would be interpreted as a sign of impotence. So, like many a weak man in a similar situation, he blusteringly rejected the demands of the people and threatened to rule even more tyrannically than his father. As a consequence the Israelites, now completely alienated from the Davidic royal house, raised the old battle cry (vs. 16) which had been previously sounded in the days of Sheba ben Bichri (II Sam. 20:1) and renounced their allegiance. Adoram (Adoniram; see 4:6), the commissar for forced labor, was stoned to death; Rehoboam was forced to flee for his life; and Jeroboam, the first hero of the resistance movement in the north, was recalled from exile in Egypt to become king of Israel. These events took place about 922 B.C. The extent of Rehoboam's loss is indicated by the fact that he was able to retain control only over his own tribe of Judah and the tribe of Benjamin, properly one of the northern tribes but immediately adjacent to Judah on the north. He had, of course, also the inestimable advantage of holding the city of Jerusalem, which lay on the border between these two tribes. According to the present account, he began to plan the military reconquest of the north, but was dissuaded from this impossible task by the prophet Shemaiah (vss. 22-24).

The Reign of Jeroboam I in Israel (12:25—14:20)

With the accession of Jeroboam, the author, or authors, of the book begin the practice which makes the reading of this middle part of Kings so confusing for the casual reader. Having introduced Jeroboam, they will follow the account of his reign through to the end; then they will go back to the history of Rehoboam and his successors, Abijam and Asa, in Judah, whose reigns were contemporary with Jeroboam's in Israel, and follow them through to the end. Since Jeroboam died during the reign of Asa, they will then return to Israel and to the successors of Jeroboam. They continue this method of alternating their stories until the fall of the Northern Kingdom. To avoid confusion the reader must note very carefully the occurrence in the narrative of the names Judah and Israel. "Judah," of course, means the Southern Kingdom, with its capital at Jerusalem, and "Israel" in this context means the Northern Kingdom, with its capital successively at Shechem, Tirzah, and Samaria (elsewhere in the Bible "Israel" is used quite commonly as a name for the entire nation, including Judah). A good practical device for keeping the histories of the two kingdoms disentangled is to draw a line in pencil or crayon beside those passages which deal with Judah.

It is important to keep in mind that during all the history of the following two centuries, Israel was by far the larger, wealthier, and more advanced of the two kingdoms. Their relative size is indicated by the fact that Israel consisted of ten tribes, while Judah consisted of but two. Israel had more people, more fertile land, more extensive contacts with the outside world; and when friendly relations were finally established between the sister states, an alliance came into being in which Israel was decidedly the dominant partner. The kings of Judah were at times little more than clients of their powerful neighbors to the north. There is considerable doubt as to which maintained the purer traditions of the old Yahweh religion. Arguments can be advanced on both sides, although we must remember that our knowledge of northern Israel comes down to us filtered through Judean sources. It is certainly significant that the prophetic movement first took its rise in the north. The greatest advantage possessed by the Southern Kingdom was the Davidic dynasty, which continued to rule in Judah to the very end, whereas the history of the Northern Kingdom is one of frequent rebellion and dynastic change. Judah was also blessed by continuing to hold the city of Jerusalem, the most important city in the land and one which was destined through the centuries to become a center of devotion for its people as no city of northern Israel was ever able to do. From the religious point of view, we should note that the treasure of Israel's religion was ultimately transmitted to the world through the agency of the insignificant kingdom of Judah rather than through the great and powerful kingdom of Israel, a further illustration of the biblical principle that God chooses "what is weak in the world to shame the strong" (I Cor. 1:27).

Jeroboam's Policies (12:25-33)

Jeroboam's first need was for a capital city. It was natural that he should first of all select the city of Shechem, which guarded the principal east and west highway of the country at the entrance to the pass between Mount Ebal and Mount Gerizim and had already played an important role in the religious and political history of the northern tribes (see Gen. 12:6-7; Gen. 33:18—

34:31; Joshua 24:1-28; Judges 9). He rebuilt and fortified the site and also fortified Penuel, directly opposite it on the other side of the Jordan, to protect its eastern approaches. Only by accident (14:17) we learn that he later transferred his capital to Tirzah, a more readily defensible site a few miles to the northeast of Shechem, which then remained the capital of Israel until it was finally replaced, under Omri, by Samaria (16:23-24).

Most of this section is devoted to Jeroboam's religious measures, which were probably not so revolutionary as the Deuteronomic history implies. The sanctuaries at Bethel near the southern borders of the kingdom and at Dan in the far north of Galilee were ancient shrines of the Hebrew people, long antedating the sanctuary at Jerusalem (see, for example, Gen. 12:8; 28:18-22; Judges 18:29-30; 20:18). The people of the north had no doubt continued to worship there even after the Temple had been built in Jerusalem. The "calves," bull-images, which Jeroboam is said to have erected, were traditional symbols of Yahweh's strength and creative power; it will be remembered that such images were to be found even in Solomon's Temple (7:25), although they did not occupy any central position in its worship. The difference in the date on which the Feast of Tabernacles was celebrated probably represents a difference in the traditions of the two parts of the country rather than a deliberate innovation on Jeroboam's part. The religious reforms of Jeroboam were an attempt to revitalize the old traditions of the northern tribes in conscious opposition to those of the south; their great danger lay in the fact that the use of bull-images in worship, however much it might be rationalized, was contrary to the best instincts of the Yahweh religion, and was a dangerous approximation to the religious practices of the Canaanites—a step in the direction of syncretism. To the Deuteronomic historians, writing more than three centuries later, Jeroboam's policies could seem like nothing other than deliberate apostasy, and they interpret them as such. In their minds all the later kings of Israel were tarred with the brush of "Jeroboam the son of Nebat . . . [who] made Israel to sin" (see, for example, 15:30, 34; 16:2, 19, 26), and they took the religious policy he instituted to be the ultimate cause for the destruction of the Northern Kingdom (II Kings 17:21). The Chronicler carries this attitude to its logical conclusion by entirely omitting the story of the apostate kingdom of Israel from his account of the history of the People of God.

A Popular Story About Jeroboam (13:1-34)

The account of Jeroboam's religious activities provides the editor with an occasion for inserting a popular tale about a prophecy which was uttered against the king even in his lifetime. This is the one extensive section in Kings which may be regarded as wholly unhistorical. It bears all the marks of a folk story and certainly represents God as acting in a way which is out of harmony with the main body of Scripture. Especially worthy of note in this connection is the mention of "Samaria" (vs. 32)—the city did not even exist at this time—and the specific prediction of Josiah's reform 300 years later, a type of prediction almost without parallel anywhere else in the Old Testament. It is likely that the story as we have it now is a product of the age in which Josiah lived, that is, the late seventh century B.C.

A Judean prophet is pictured as coming to Jeroboam while the latter was offering incense on the altar at Bethel. The prophet predicts the defilement of this altar. When the king attempts to have the man arrested, his arm suddenly withers and the altar is miraculously demolished. The king's arm is restored at the intercession of the prophet, who, however, refuses to accept either a gift or the proffer of hospitality, since his commission from Yahweh forbade him while on his journey to hold any social intercourse with the men of the north. The story then is complicated by the introduction of a northern prophet (vs. 11) who entices the man from the south to eat a meal with him by falsely asserting that this had been ordered by a special message from the Lord (vs.18). Since the southern prophet has now disobeyed his original commission—although with the best intentions—he has laid himself open to punishment, as his northern counterpart somewhat unkindly announces to him (vss. 21-22), and on the way back to Judah he is killed by a lion (vs. 24). The northern prophet then arranges a decent burial for him in his own tomb and orders that when he himself dies his body shall be buried beside that of the man from the south. The moral of the latter part of this tale seems to be the necessity of absolute obedience to God's commands, but since the disobedience of the Judean prophet was entirely innocent—as he had no reason to suspect the other prophet of lying—the lesson is lost on the modern reader. The story is interesting for the insight it gives into a certain type of popular religion which operated on a far lower level than that

of the great teachers of Israel, and which is worth preserving for
that reason, but we may be grateful that there is so little of this
kind of thing in the Bible. The lesson of obedience is an important
one, but certainly God does not deliberately mislead his children,
as the story may seem to imply, nor does he tear them to pieces
with wild animals for unwitting sins. The great religious teachers
of Israel were quite as sure on this point as we are.

Another Story of Prophecy; Jeroboam's Death (14:1-20)

The story told at the beginning of this chapter is more securely
rooted in history than the one in chapter 13, but it has obviously
been retold by the Deuteronomic editors of Kings in such a way
as to bring out explicitly their interpretation of Israel's history.
In this story we meet again the prophet Ahijah from Shiloh, who
was said to have predicted and perhaps instigated Jeroboam's successful revolt against the Davidic dynasty (11:29-39). Here, however, he plays a different role. Far from appearing as a friend of
Jeroboam, he is an avowed critic and prophesies the ultimate destruction of his house and his kingdom. It is of course quite possible that in the course of the years Ahijah had been alienated by
the king's religious policies, perhaps specifically by the choice of
Bethel instead of Shiloh as one of the principal northern shrines.
In any event, when Jeroboam's wife came disguised to the prophet
at Shiloh to learn what would be the outcome of her son's serious
illness, the prophet, who had no difficulty in recognizing her, announced that the child would die as soon as she returned home
(vs. 12). And not only that; he also took advantage of the opportunity (according to the present form of the story) to prophesy
the imminent destruction of the dynasty of Jeroboam (vss. 7-10,
14) and the eventual exile of all the inhabitants of northern Israel to Assyria as a punishment for Jeroboam's religious policies
(vs. 15). This is a statement of the philosophy of the final editors
of the Books of Kings, who were certain that the disasters which
befell both the Northern and the Southern Kingdoms were the result of their persistent disloyalty toward the God of Israel and his
righteous demands. This philosophy, in turn, is a practical appli-
cation to the history of Israel of the specific teachings of the Book
of Deuteronomy (28:15-19, 36-68; 30:15-20) and of the great
prophets who inspired it (see, for example, Amos 3:13—4:3;
Hosea 4:1-3). The Asherim of verse 15 were some kind of cult
objects, probably wooden poles representing a Canaanite goddess

of fertility, which were set up in the sanctuaries. At the conclusion of the story we learn, quite incidentally (vs. 17), that the royal capital had been transferred from Shechem to Tirzah, where it would remain during the next four reigns.

Verses 19 and 20 contain the formula which, with some variations, the Deuteronomic historians use at the end of their account of each of the kings. Notice the mention of their source book, a copy of the "Chronicles of the Kings of Israel" (see Introduction).

The Disastrous Reign of Rehoboam in Judah (14:21-31)

The story now returns to Judah and the reigns of the three successors of Solomon. In verses 21-24 we have a typical introductory formula of the Deuteronomic editors of the book. These introductory and concluding formulas (see vss. 29-31) give a certain unavoidably monotonous character to considerable stretches of the Books of Kings. It is evident that Rehoboam's religious policy was no improvement on that of his father and was not essentially different from that of Jeroboam, except that it was attached to the sanctuary of Jerusalem rather than to Dan or Bethel and did not involve the use of bull-images. The worship of the God of Israel still continued in Judah at the local "high places," which were so freighted with memories of the old Canaanite gods that it was difficult sometimes to distinguish the worship of Yahweh from that of Baal. Here the Hebrews continued to venerate the rude stone pillars, the wooden Asherim (see comment on verse 15), and the sacred trees which were an inheritance from the Canaanites. Worst of all, here the sacred prostitutes continued to ply their trade. The most objectionable feature of the old Canaanite religion had been its morbid encouragement of sexual practices, both normal and abnormal, which were believed to stimulate the fertility of the land. In the country districts at least, these practices were often adopted wholesale in the religion of Yahweh—a tendency against which the great prophets would contend vigorously and which would finally be brought to an end when the reform of Josiah abolished the country shrines and permitted the worship of Yahweh only in the Temple at Jerusalem.

The most important external event in the reign of Rehoboam was the invasion under Shishak (properly, Sheshonk), the first ruler of a new Egyptian dynasty, who took advantage of the weakness of the now divided Hebrew people to raid their lands. On the walls of the great temple of Karnak in Egypt he has left a record of this event and there reports that it included attacks upon cities in both Judah and Israel. The plundering of the Temple treasury and of the golden shields from the House of the Forest of Lebanon (compare 10:17) is a token of the fading glory of Solomon's kingdom. Verse 30 reports that border skirmishes with Israel continued throughout Rehoboam's reign.

The Short Reign of Abijam in Judah (15:1-8)

In II Chronicles 13:1 this king's name is given as "Abijah," a more orthodox name, but for that reason perhaps less likely to be correct. The name of his mother is also given differently. Nothing is recorded of his brief reign of three years beyond the fact that his religious policy was unchanged from that of his father. As a result this whole section consists almost entirely of the customary introductory and concluding formulas of the Deuteronomic editors. The continuing conflict with Israel is briefly noted in verse 7; the Chronicler has at this point a long account of a decisive defeat supposedly administered on Jeroboam by Judean armies, but it hardly sounds authentic (II Chron. 13:3-21).

The Reforming Reign of Asa in Judah (15:9-24)

In both kingdoms there were always conservative groups which opposed the syncretistic (see the comment on 11:1-40) religious policies of their rulers and advocated a return to the simple and virile traditions of the older days. In the declining years of the nation their point of view would receive immortal expression in the words of the great prophets, but even before that time they sometimes obtained sufficient influence in the court to effect a change in policy, as they did in Israel in the time of Elisha, and in Judah during the reigns of Asa and Jehoshaphat. In the case of Asa we have no indication in Kings that the reform was the result of any influence beyond that of the king himself, but it can hardly be doubted that some outstanding prophetic personality on the pattern of Nathan, Ahijah, or Shemaiah must have been the power behind the throne. The Chronicler gives us the name of such a prophet, Azariah the son of Oded, and attributes the king's actions to his preaching (II Chron. 15:1-8), but the historical character of the account is sometimes questioned. The vigor of Asa's reform is shown by the fact that he deposed the queen mother—frequently a powerful figure in an oriental court—because she was the chief support of the "liberal," syncretizing party. She was evidently a particular devotee of Asherah (vs. 13), a well-known goddess from the Canaanite pantheon. Asa had the image of Asherah burned in the Kidron Valley, which separates Jerusalem from the Mount of Olives to the east. Although he abolished the sacred prostitutes, it is specifically said that he did not take the radical step, eventually taken by Josiah, of abolishing all worship at the country shrines, the "high places."

The other important event of Asa's reign was his decisive, if limited, victory over Baasha the king of Israel (vss. 16-22). Baasha will be formally introduced later in the chapter (vss. 27, 33), but the method of the historians requires the preliminary mention of his name here. Baasha prosecuted the continuing struggle against the Southern Kingdom by establishing a fortress at Ramah, only a few miles north of Jerusalem. Since this would have brought the southern border of Israel uncomfortably close to Judah's capital city, Asa determined to secure help from an outside source. By bribery (using part of the Temple treasury) he succeeded in forming a military alliance with Ben-hadad, king of the recently established Syrian state which centered in Damascus (see 11:23-25 for the story of its founding). While Baasha was still busy at Ramah on his southern borders, Ben-hadad created a diversion by invading Galilee to the north (vs. 20) and forced the Israelite king to withdraw. Asa then seized Ramah and with the building materials Baasha had collected built two Judean forts at nearby sites to protect his frontier from further attacks from Israel. While Asa's move was a clever one, and highly successful, it would certainly have brought upon him the reprobation of the later great prophets, who were opposed on principle to foreign alliances of this kind (see, for example, Hosea 7:11-12; Isa. 30:1-5; Jer. 2:36-37), believing that a nation should put its trust in God rather than in force of arms or political maneuverings. As a matter of fact, the Syrians, who were thus first invited onto Israel's soil by the gold of a Judean king, would return frequently during the two following centuries to plague both the kingdoms (see 20:1; 22:1; II Kings 6:8, 24; 9:14; Isa. 7:1).

The Brief Reign of Nadab in Israel (15:25-32)

The turbulence which continually interrupted the dynastic succession in Israel in contrast to the internal peace enjoyed by the house of David in Judah is strikingly illustrated by the fate of the second king of the Northern Kingdom. Nadab, the son of Jeroboam I, succeeded in holding his throne for only two years, at the end of which an upstart, Baasha, taking advantage of Nadab's military preoccupation with the Philistines, engineered a revolt which unseated his master and put himself in power. As was customary, Nadab and his whole family were murdered in order to make sure that no avengers and no legitimate claimants to the throne would be left. Thus the dynasty of Jeroboam lasted only for parts of two generations. For the Deuteronomists, this was the well-merited punishment of Jeroboam's apostasy (vs. 30).

The Reigns of Baasha, Elah, and Zimri in Israel (15:33—16:22)

The Deuteronomists found nothing of particular interest to record from Baasha's reign of twenty-four years (15:33—16:7) beyond the fact of his unsuccessful campaign against Asa, which they have already related in 15:16-22. Since he was a northern king, he was to their minds obviously a bad one, and they report a prophecy against him of precisely the same character as that against his first predecessor, Jeroboam. The prophet Jehu, who is mentioned here (16:1), is named by the Chronicler as the author of one of his source books (II Chron. 20:34). Tirzah is now explicitly designated as the capital of Israel (15:33; compare 14:17 and 15:21, where the name occurs only incidentally).

The fate of Baasha's dynasty was destined to be the same as that of Jeroboam. Elah, the son of Baasha, after a reign of two years, was assassinated by Zimri, one of the officers of his army. Apparently he well deserved his fate since he was engaged in a drunken debauch (vs. 9) while his armies were fighting against the Philistines (vs. 15). In monotonous accord with custom, all the members of his family were destroyed also.

Zimri, although listed as a king of Israel, hardly deserves the name, since his reign lasted for only a week and ended in flaming disaster when Omri, the commander-in-chief of the army, took the field against him (vss. 15-20). After his death there was civil war for three years between the partisans of Omri and Tibni, but at length Omri prevailed and was recognized as legitimate king of Israel.

The Important Reign of Omri in Israel (16:23-28)

It has often been noted that the Deuteronomists unintentionally present a somewhat distorted picture of the actual course of events because their purpose was not so much to relate Israel's history as to give a religious interpretation of it. Consequently they sometimes give a great deal of space to things, such as the building of Solomon's Temple, which have great religious interest, and pass over lightly other things which have no such significance but are of outstanding importance judged by the standards of secular history. The reign of Omri is a good example: so important was his reign in the eyes of contemporaries that for many generations the kingdom of Israel was known to the Assyrians simply as "The Land of the House of Omri." The lack of any interesting religious developments caused the Deuteronomists to dismiss it in five verses, consisting for the most part of their customary clichés.

Plainly a very capable ruler, he founded a dynasty which lasted nearly forty years (Ahab, Ahaziah, and Jehoram all being of his line). Only one accomplishment is recorded of him here—the establishment of the new capital city of Samaria. This was an event of prime moment, since for the first time Israel would have a capital of the commanding importance of Jerusalem in the south —an easily defended city, beautifully located on a hilltop in a fertile valley (see Isa. 28:1). Its name would eventually be extended to the whole territory of Israel, whose inhabitants would be known simply as Samaritans. Under the Greeks, King Herod, and the Romans, Samaria would remain one of the chief cities of Palestine. Fine buildings from all periods of its existence have been uncovered and much light thrown upon its history by modern archaeological investigation.

From the famous Mesha Stone (see the comment on II Kings 3:4-27) we learn that Omri also conquered the land of Moab and added it to Israel's domain.

The Critical Reign of Ahab in Israel (16:29—22:40)

However cavalierly the Deuteronomists deal with Omri, they fully compensate by the space they allot to his son Ahab, whose reign they justly reckon to be the most significant from a religious point of view in the history of northern Israel. In the time of Ahab and Jezebel, the long-smoldering opposition between those who supported tolerant, syncretistic religious policies inaugurated by Solomon and the adherents of the ancient and distinctive religion of Israel broke out into an open conflict which finally resulted in the overthrow of Omri's dynasty and a decisive victory for the conservative party. Because of their exclusively religious interests, the historians of the Books of Kings ignore Ahab's secular accomplishments, especially his participation with Syrian allies in the important battle of Karkar against the Assyrians (853 B.C.), a fact of which we learn only from the inscription of the Assyrian king, Shalmaneser III, who reports that "Ahab the Israelite" contributed 2,000 chariots and 10,000 men.

Ahab's Accession and Marriage to Jezebel (16:29-34)

Quite as famous as Ahab himself is Jezebel, his queen, a strong-minded Phoenician princess who was determined to introduce into Israel the worship of Baal-Melkart, the patron deity of her own people. Ahab continued to be a worshiper of the national God of Israel (as is evidenced by the fact that all the children of Ahab and Jezebel have Yahweh names: Ahaz-*iah, Jeho*-ram, Athal-*iah*), but, like Solomon, he was indulgent toward the religion of his wife and erected a private chapel for her god. The difference between the time of Solomon and that of Ahab lay in the personality of Jezebel, who was not content with the private worship of Melkart but wished to incorporate him into the official cult of the kingdom of Israel.

Verse 34 records the fact that Jericho, which had existed only as a small settlement since Joshua's conquest, was rebuilt as a city in Ahab's time. Fatal accidents which apparently befell the youngest and oldest sons of the builder were interpreted as a fulfillment of the curse laid upon the site by Joshua (Joshua 6:26).

The Flight of Elijah; His Sojourn in Phoenicia (17:1-24)

With chapter 17, the whole mood of the First Book of Kings suddenly changes. For the most part the style of the previous chapters has been dry, factual, somewhat monotonous; but as soon as Elijah appears on the scene the narrative becomes warm, vigorous, alive, and full of interest. There can be no doubt that the editors of the book are now making use of a different source, no longer the official records ("the Chronicles") of the kings of Judah and Israel, but a book of popular stories about the two great prophets Elijah and Elisha. The style is racy and the content exciting. Fortunately it also appears to contain good historical material, even though there has been a certain dramatic heightening of some of the events and the characters are portrayed in vivid contrasts of black and white with no pale shades of gray to dull the reader's enthusiasm.

Although he left no book behind him, Elijah was certainly the first of the major prophets and one who understands him will understand the others also. Coming from the land of Gilead in Transjordan, nearer the edge of the desert than most of Israel, he must have been in closer touch with the old traditions of the God of Moses and the Fathers. The luxuries, injustices, and religious indifference of the court at Samaria would have been more offensive to him than to those who had grown up in the more "civilized" country west of the Jordan. Indeed, these things were, to him, not merely offensive but intolerable, and he devoted his life to single-minded and largely single-handed battle against them. Nothing is told us in the present narrative of his parents, his early history, or how he came to accept the challenge presented by Ahab and his foreign queen. The original biography must have given some information on these points, but the editor of Kings chooses to introduce his hero suddenly, without warning, like a flash of lightning in a cloudless sky. With no hint of preparation Elijah abruptly appears upon the stage announcing to the king the coming of a drought over the whole land as a punishment for his policies and a warning to change them. No sooner has he pronounced the curse than he vanishes as mysteriously as he came. For a while he lives in solitude in his own country, east of the Jordan, where, by the Brook Cherith, he is miraculously fed by the birds of heaven. But when the drought causes even the brook to dry up, he moves to Phoenicia (vs. 8), strangely enough the very land from which Jezebel came. There he took up his residence with a widow to whose advantage he was able to use his wonder-working powers. Since Phoenicia, too, was affected by the drought and the famine which followed, he rewarded the widow's hospitality by providing her with an unfailing jar of meal and an inexhaustible jug of oil. When, later on, the widow's son died, she interpreted the disaster, in accordance with the popular theology of the time, as punishment for some fault she had com-

mitted. Even the prophet felt that God had acted in an unreason-
able and arbitrary way (vs. 20). Nevertheless he carried the body
up to his little chamber on the roof, approached no doubt by an
outside stairway, and there restored the boy to life. The word
"soul" in verse 21 should rather be translated "life," since the
Hebrews had no conception of "the soul" in the usual modern
sense of the term.

Even the casual reader will have noticed a curious similarity
between some of the stories told about Elijah and those told about
Elisha (compare especially this story with II Kings 4:8-37). It
seems probable that there is some confusion in the tradition. Different as were the characters and careers of the two men, they
were sufficiently similar for the same stories to seem appropriate
to both. In the long period of oral transmission, before the narrative was written down, it would have been easy for a story told
about one prophet to be unintentionally transferred to the other.

In the Gospels, Jesus quotes the story of Elijah's service to the
widow as evidence that a prophet, who is often unacceptable to
his own people, may, of necessity, have to exercise his ministry
among foreigners (Luke 4:24-26). The Elijah story thus becomes
a kind of prophecy of Jesus' ministry to the Gentiles. It is interesting to recall that Jesus himself visited this same region during his only visit to Gentile lands (Mark 7:24-30).

Elijah Returns to Israel (18:1-19)

After three years of drought, during which Ahab had vainly
sought to find Elijah, the prophet was impelled by the Lord to return to his own country. There he encountered Obadiah, the chief
steward of the king and a loyal worshiper of the Lord, who had
befriended some of the Lord's prophets during a persecution by
Jezebel. Although Obadiah had a special commission to locate
Elijah, he was afraid at first to report his success, because of the
prophet's reputation for sudden appearances and disappearances.
But, convinced at last by Elijah's pledge, he reported to the king
that he had found him, so Ahab and the prophet met once again.
This time Elijah insisted, as a condition for ending the drought,
that there must be a trial of strength between the Lord and Baal-
Melkart to determine once and for all which should be the God
of Israel.

In verse 12, the word "Spirit" could just as well be translated
"wind"; the Hebrew words are the same and it is often difficult to

tell which translation gives the more accurate sense in English. In verse 18, "the Baals" means other gods than Yahweh, especially the local fertility gods of Canaan. In the Elijah story, "Baal" in the *singular* means specifically Melkart, the city god of Tyre. Notice, in verse 19, that Baal, unlike Yahweh, has a female counterpart, the goddess Asherah. This pairing of gods and goddesses is characteristic of fertility religions and was especially abhorrent to the Hebrews, whose language does not even have a word for goddess.

The Contest on Mount Carmel (18:20-46)

In modern thought the word "prophet" is applied chiefly to one who has the ability to see into the future. While ancient prophets often laid claim to this power, it was not the essence of their office. They were simply devotees of the deity, usually living at his shrine, capable at times of being "possessed" in a mysterious way by his spirit and, when occasion required, of delivering his message. The state of "possession" was sometimes spontaneous, sometimes artificially stimulated by music and dancing (I Sam. 10:5; II Kings 3:15) or, as in the present account of the prophets of Baal, by self-mutilation (vs. 28). In addition to these "ecstatic" prophets who lived in communities (of whom Elisha was plainly one), there were occasional solitary prophets like Elijah and the great prophets of later times, who operated mainly by themselves and with whom the phenomenon of "possession" or "ecstasy" played a much less important role.

Both Yahweh and Baal-Melkart had prophets attached to their cult, and the contest here described took place between them. The scene of the contest was the headland of Mount Carmel, which juts out boldly onto the Mediterranean coast just south of the modern city of Haifa; it was undoubtedly an ancient "high place" devoted to the worship of Yahweh as well as the older gods of the land. Melkart's prophets numbered 450; Yahweh's, it is said, but one. (One naturally wonders what had become of the hundred mentioned in verses 4 and 13, but this is not the kind of question one is expected to ask in a popular story of this kind; Elijah's claim to stand alone must be taken as dramatic hyperbole.) The prophets of Baal were given the first opportunity to show the power of their god, and they exerted themselves to the utmost of their ability while Elijah stood by and made fun of them (vss. 26-29). These verses give a vivid picture of the way an an-

cient band of prophets engaged in the worship of their god, dancing in a peculiar manner (like the modern whirling dervishes),
crying out, cutting themselves with knives, and acting like mad-
men. The bands of Yahweh-prophets whom we occasionally meet
in the early years of the kingdom (I Sam. 19:20; II Kings 2:3)
no doubt behaved in much the same way. Elijah, though, will
have none of this. He makes the test as difficult as possible by
pouring water over the sacrifice and then, in simple dignity, asks
for God's sign of approval. A flash of lightning strikes the altar
and completely destroys it, leaving in no one's mind any doubt
that Yahweh truly is God in Israel. There follows the horrifying
scene in which Elijah slaughters the 450 devotees of Baal (vs.
40). Finally, at the end of the chapter, the clouds appear, the
rains return, and the drought is broken. Only then does the prophetic "ecstasy" come upon Elijah (vs. 46: "the hand of the LORD"
was on him), but in its power he races Ahab's chariot nearly
twenty miles back to the royal estate at Jezreel.

This story is certainly one of the masterpieces of world literature. With all its atmosphere of early, almost barbaric religion,
its central message is as valid today as ever. The true God is a
jealous God; he will have no other gods before him. One chooses
to be either for him or against him. The challenge of Elijah is
a challenge to the heart of every man: "How long will you go
limping with two different opinions? If the LORD is God, follow
him; but if Baal, then follow him" (vs. 21). The decision *must* be
made.

The Epistle of James finds in this long story of Elijah and the
drought a significant example of the power of intercessory prayer
(James 5:17-18).

Elijah at Mount Horeb (19:1-18)

One might suppose from the previous chapter that the struggle
was over. Actually, the contest at Carmel was only an incident.
The final victory was still far in the future and would not come
until the days of Elisha (II Kings 10:18-28). In the meantime,
whatever temporary advantage Elijah might seem to have won
by his success on Mount Carmel was cancelled by the renewed
antagonism of Jezebel, who put the prophet in fear of his life.
Leaving the territory of the kingdom of Israel, Elijah traveled to
Beer-sheba in the kingdom of Judah, at the extreme south of
ancient Israelite Palestine, and then went a day's journey into

the desert beyond. There, in dejection, he sat down in the inadequate shade of a broom shrub and longed for death. But his great work had only just begun, and the Lord, who once had fed him by the help of the ravens, sent an angel to cheer him on. Food and drink were provided and Elijah was strengthened for the long trip over the desert to the Mount of God, where once Moses had received the Law and acted as intermediary in the establishment of the Covenant between the Lord and the people of Israel. According to the tradition current in Judah, the name of the mountain was Sinai; but in Israel its name was Horeb. The most primitive view pictured God as actually living on the mountain and having to travel across the wilderness when he came to help his people (Deut. 33:2; Judges 5:4-5), but by Elijah's time this conception was no longer current. Nevertheless Horeb was, for Israel, the most sacred spot in the world, a place where God was certainly to be found in a special way. So it was natural for Elijah to go there to hold communion with the God of his ancestors and to renew his own flagging courage. "Forty days and forty nights" is a conventional phrase meaning simply "a long time" (compare Exod. 24:18; Mark 1:13).

On arrival at the mountain, Elijah took up residence in a cave and there at length held converse with the God in whose service he had risked his life. The story is both vividly dramatic and theologically profound. As Elijah stands upon the mountainside, his senses are assaulted in turn by a wind of terrifying force, by an earthquake, and by a fire. But all these natural forces, traditional signs of the presence of Israel's God (see Pss. 18:7-10; 29:3-9), are here merely the advance heralds of his approach. He himself was manifested by "a still small voice," "the soft whisper," "the sound of a gentle silence" (as the Hebrew phrase may be variously translated) which followed the violent disturbances of nature. Only then did the prophet cover his face in reverence and listen for the divine message. God commissioned him to return to Israel and there continue his reforming work. The original commission was probably given only in general terms; what now appears in verses 15-18 is an elaboration which recapitulates the events that actually followed. Three points are mentioned: (1) Revolution is to be fomented in Syria, and also (2) in Israel; (3) Elisha is to be chosen as Elijah's successor. As a matter of fact, this is really Elisha's program rather than Elijah's; Elijah accomplished only number 3 and made no effort to carry out points 1 and 2. Verse 18 is important because there appears in it, for the first time in the Bible, the doctrine of "the remnant"—that is, the doctrine that no matter how apostate the nation as a whole may become, there will always be a small but faithful remnant on which God can build for the future (see the comment on II Kings 19:30-31).

The Call of Elisha (19:19-21)

The town of Abel-meholah, where Elisha lived (vs. 16), was probably a town in Transjordan (Gilead), the same part of the country from which Elijah came. Evidently Elisha belonged to a wealthy family since he is represented as having twelve yoke of oxen at work simultaneously in his field. The mantle which Elijah cast upon him was a badge of the prophetic calling, as we learn from II Kings 1:8; Zechariah 13:4; and Matthew 3:4. After having accepted the mantle, Elisha asks for permission to say good-by to his father and mother, and apparently Elijah gives him permission to do so, although the meaning of his words is not very plain either in English or in Hebrew. The final act was the slaughter of Elisha's yoke of oxen as a sacrifice in honor of the solemnity of the occasion. The adventures of Elisha are not resumed until II Kings 2:1.

It is sometimes supposed, because of the similarity of the names in English and the obvious confusion in some of the stories about them, that Elijah and Elisha were merely slightly variant names for the same person. In Hebrew, though, the names are quite different in sound, spelling, and meaning. Elijah means "My God is Yahweh" (a very appropriate name for Yahweh's chief protagonist), while Elisha means "My God is salvation." Not only are the names different, but, as we shall see, the characters and programs of the two men are so different that there is no possibility of any basic confusion, even though stories originally told about one have occasionally been told about the other also.

Ahab's Victory Over the Syrians (20:1-43)

The story of Elijah continues in chapter 21. Before we reach that, however, we are introduced to a different source, and to an important episode in the almost continuous war which was going on between Israel and Syria. In the chapters which follow, several such episodes appear (for example, I Kings 22 and II Kings 6:24—7:20), but their chronological relationship to each other and to the periods of peace which occasionally intervened is frequently uncertain, nor is it by any means always clear just why they have been introduced into the narrative at the points where we now find them.

The beginning of the present chapter finds the city of Samaria besieged by the Syrians under Ben-hadad (there seems to have been more than one king of this name). Ahab, driven to despair, offered to surrender, but the Syrian king overplayed his hand and insisted upon terms so harsh that Ahab, on the advice of his council, refused to accept them. Ben-hadad, still unduly confident, did not take seriously the little commando force which Ahab first sent out (vss. 15-19) so the apparently small group he dispatched to meet it was killed to a man (vs. 20). Confusion then broke out in the Syrian camp, and Ahab, dashing out with the larger force he was holding in reserve (vs. 15b), put the whole army of besiegers to ignominious rout (vs. 21). Some light is thrown upon the popular theology of the ancient Near East by the opinion of the Syrian king that the gods of the Hebrews were mountain gods, whose worshipers might therefore be more readily defeated in the plain (vss. 23-25), but the God of Israel quickly vindicated himself as a God of universal power at a second battle the following season (vss. 29-30). The location of Aphek, where this battle was fought, is uncertain, but it was at least on level land, possibly in the region east of the Sea of Galilee. Ben-hadad was so thoroughly defeated that he simply threw himself on the mercy of his brother king in Israel (vss. 31-33), who, it is interesting to note, belonged to a nation whose kings had a reputation for mildness (vs. 31). Some incidental information about previous relations between Syria and Israel is obtained from verse 34, which reveals that Omri, Ahab's father, had been forced to cede territory and commercial rights in Samaria to the Syrians (unless the reference is really to Baasha and the incident mentioned in 15:19, in which case the word "father" would have to be understood in a very loose sense). Ahab regained most of the lost lands and won for his people trading rights in the bazaars of Damascus. A treaty was then signed between the two kings.

It is evident that in this source Ahab is regarded in a distinctly favorable light. He is courageous, resourceful, merciful, and receives support and guidance from prophets of the Lord (vss. 13-14, 22, 28). This view of him is in striking contrast to that of the Elijah-Elisha source, where he appears to be without redeeming traits. This is confirmation of the fact that the Elijah-Elisha source is marked by a tendency toward oversimplification and dramatic heightening. Ahab was a far more complex character than he seems to be in those somewhat biased accounts. But the generally favorable attitude of even the present source has been altered at the end by the editorial insertion of a prophetic story in which Ahab is roundly condemned, not for his religious apostasy, as in the Elijah-Elisha stories, but for his merciful treatment of the king of Syria, whom he set free when he might have killed him (vss. 35-43). This unpleasant tale seems to have originated in the same circles as chapter 13 (compare 20:36 with 13:24).

The story of Ahab's Syrian wars is continued in chapter 22.

Elijah, Ahab, and Naboth's Vineyard (21:1-29)

Probably no one in Old Testament times believed that religion could be divorced from politics, business, or economic life in general. The idea that life can be divided up into separate, mutually exclusive compartments is essentially a modern one. For men of the Bible, life was a unit. Looked at from one point of view it was altogether concerned with a man's individual relationship with God; from another it consisted of the relationship of one man with others within the framework of a community; and from yet another it was the relationship of God with the whole community of men. But these relationships were all interlocking and were woven together into a single, indivisible whole. Every "religion" implied—as indeed it still does—a certain kind of social life among men. So whether men worshiped the Lord or Baal was not simply a matter of choosing between two different creeds, but of choosing between two different types of social system. The knowledge that this was so was certainly a strong element in Jezebel's drive to introduce the worship of the Phoenician Baal-Melkart among the people of Israel. She despised the simple, backward, "democratic" ways (to borrow a modern term) of the people among whom she had come to live, and she wished to impose upon them the autocratic government to which she was accustomed and which was characteristic of the other civilized nations of the ancient Near Eastern world. But this same knowledge was also an important element in the resistance which Elijah and his followers offered to her program. Yahweh was not merely the ancestral God of the Hebrews; he was also the defender of Israel's traditional social system and of the laws which governed it.

So Elijah's conflict with the royal family over Naboth and his vineyard was not merely an incident in the larger struggle but an integral part of it. If one aspect of the struggle, that which *we* should call purely "religious," is dramatized in the story of the contest on Mount Carmel, the other aspect, the "social," is dramatized by the story of Naboth's vineyard. For both Elijah and Jezebel, as well as for all the later prophets, these were not two different things, but merely two phases of a single, indivisible battle in which there could never be any compromise or partial solution.

Jezreel, situated in the fertile Plain of Esdraelon, seems to have been a kind of second capital for the Northern Kingdom. Here, at any rate, the king had a palace and a splendid estate. Immediately adjoining it was the vineyard of Naboth, a common citizen. This was a choice piece of ground, admirably situated to round out the king's holdings, but, unfortunately for Ahab, the property was understood by Hebrew custom to belong to the whole family of Naboth, past and future, and not merely to Naboth himself. The ownership of land was the chief safeguard of the independence of the family unit and was therefore inalienable under Israelite law. So Naboth refused either to sell or to trade the vineyard. Notice that he invokes the name of the God of Israel in doing so (vs. 3). The incident is a striking one and reveals much about the spirit of Old Testament religion: the simple citizen defies the king and the king can only return to his palace and sulk about it. This situation was intolerable to Jezebel, so, even though she does not venture to challenge the laws of the Hebrew community directly, she concocts a plot which makes it possible for the king indirectly to attain his end. She hired false witnesses —two being necessary under Hebrew law (Deut. 17:6; Matt. 26:60)—to accuse Naboth of having cursed both God and the king, and then she had a public fast proclaimed to underline the serious character of the charge. To understand how serious it was one must remember that to the ancient mind a curse was not merely a form of words but a powerful magic weapon, the effects of which could be obviated only by equally powerful counter-measures. (See in 2:8-9 David's order that Shimei be destroyed for having uttered just such a curse.) Since a curse against God is too dreadful even to be mentioned, the Hebrew Bible has substituted the word "bless" euphemistically where the English text in verses 10 and 13 says "curse." Jezebel's plot was successful;

Naboth was executed (and, according to II Kings 9:26, his sons also) by an act of the whole community; so, in default of heirs, property reverted to the crown.

It was only at this point that Elijah appeared upon the stage. Few scenes in literature are more dramatic than Ahab's confrontation in the vineyard by the rough, terrifying figure of the prophet of the Lord. " 'Have you found me, O my enemy?' He answered, 'I have found you, because you have sold yourself to do what is evil in the sight of the Lord' " (vs. 20). The detailed prophecy which follows is probably a later expansion of Elijah's speech in the light of what actually happened, but no one would doubt that the denunciation was vigorous or that Elijah threatened the complete extermination of Ahab's family. The narrative concludes with an account—plausible enough in view of the fact that Ahab was a worshiper of the Lord—of the king's repentance for his violation of the laws of God and the customs of Israel. It is said that the judgment pronounced against him was somewhat ameliorated because of this (vss. 27-29). No such repentance or amelioration is recorded for Jezebel.

The story is an excellent one to remember in connection with the study of the later prophets. Elijah's uncompromising devotion to the Lord, his courage and forthrightness even before the king, and his coupling of religion and a passion for social justice are typical of them all (compare, for example, Isa. 1:16-17; Amos 5:24; Micah 3:9-12). Ahab was not the last to increase his estates at the expense of the poor, nor was he the last to be denounced for doing so (Isa. 5:8; Micah 2:1-2).

Elijah's adventures are continued in II Kings 1.

Micaiah's Prophecy of Doom: The Death of Ahab (22:1-40)

The first part of chapter 22 seems to be a continuation of the story of the Syrian wars which began in chapter 20. If the narrative is continuous, the treaty mentioned in 20:34 would appear to have remained in effect for three years. But still there lurked in the mind of Ahab a certain regret that he had not recovered the old Israelite city of Ramoth-gilead in northern Transjordan, and the story opens with a consultation on the feasibility of trying to regain it by force. Jehoshaphat, the king of Judah, officially introduced in verse 41, appears in the story as an ally, if not almost a vassal, of the king of Israel, so we must conclude that the long conflict between the kingdoms had at last ended with at least a moral victory for the preponderant power of Israel. Since the favor of the Deity was quite as important an element in battle as superiority in arms, a great band of prophets was brought together and asked to discover whether or not God would favor the enterprise. The venal character of many of these professional prophets, who lived by the bounty of the king, is revealed by their readiness to support what they understood to be the king's desire. They unanimously prophesied victory (vs. 6), and one of them fashioned iron horns with which he illustrated theatrically the manner in which the Syrians would be destroyed (vs. 11). But Jehoshaphat was suspicious of such unanimity and asked if there were not some other, solitary prophet—someone like Elijah, though he does not mention him by name—who might give a more honest judgment. There was such a prophet, Micaiah ben Imlah, but Ahab hesitated to consult him because his message was usually distasteful. Nevertheless, urged by Jehoshaphat, he at last consented to summon him. An effort was made beforehand to induce Micaiah to give the same opinion as the other prophets (vs. 13), but he insisted that he would speak only what he believed the Lord wanted him to speak. Once in the king's presence, he first mocked him by pretending to agree with the others, but, when rebuked by Ahab, he spoke the plain truth as he saw it. Such a battle as that proposed could issue only in disaster (vs. 17).

In a passage which is very important for understanding how the prophets conceived of their powers, Micaiah explains that in his vision he had been present at a meeting of God's heavenly council, where Ahab's doom was determined upon and a way devised by which he could be led to seek it out himself. A "lying spirit" had taken possession of all the king's prophets and caused them to speak false oracles of victory. Especially interesting are the ideas that God has a heavenly council (compare Job 1:6) and that false prophecies are not necessarily the result of a prophet's intention to deceive, but may come from a power outside himself—even from the Lord. The last is a possibility to which we, as Christians, could hardly assent, but the problem of explaining the fact of true and false prophecy and of distinguishing between them was undoubtedly a serious one to the ancient Hebrews and, in a sense, remains so. It still is true that a false prophet, preacher, or teacher may not be deliberately false. While no test for distinguishing them is infallible, the best is the one suggested by this story: a false prophet usually tells his audience what they *want* to hear, while a true prophet tells them what they *ought* to hear. The true prophet, in other words, is one who is likely to make his audience uncomfortable (compare Isa. 30:9-10; Jer. 6:13-14).

Micaiah was rewarded for the honesty of his answer by being put in the guardhouse until the battle, already determined upon, was over. The day went as Micaiah had predicted. In spite of an elaborate attempt at disguise, Ahab was killed and his army defeated. The story of Ahab's reign then concludes with the customary formula of the Deuteronomic editors (vss. 39-40). The reference to his "ivory house" remained problematical down to recent times, but the archaeological excavation of Samaria has brought to light a remarkable store of small, beautifully executed ivory panels, which were probably used as inlays in the furniture of the royal palace. This is no doubt the source of the name. (The ivory houses are also referred to in Amos 3:15 and Psalm 45:8.)

The Good Reign of Jehoshaphat in Judah (22:41-50)

With the death of Ahab, the editors of Kings turn back briefly to pick up the thread of history in Judah. Jehoshaphat, like his father Asa, has their complete approval, in spite of his alliance with Ahab (22:4), which was sealed by the marriage of his son Jehoram to Ahab's daughter, Athaliah (II Kings 8:18; II Chron. 18:1). From verse 47 we learn that he succeeded in regaining control over Edom, which had been lost since the days of Solomon (11:14-22). He was, therefore, in a position once more to exploit the Red Sea trade, but an unfortunate accident frustrated his attempt to do so. Furthermore he refused to accept a partnership with Israel in this purely Judean enterprise, no doubt because he feared that the interests of his own people would suffer damage, although II Kings 3:6-7 makes it clear that he continued to be Israel's military ally. The Chronicler has a great deal more to tell about Jehoshaphat's reign (II Chron. 17-20) and, though it is retold in his characteristic style and with his usual prolixity, some of his information seems reliable. Of special interest are his notes on Jehoshaphat's efforts at the religious education of the nation, his peaceful relations with other peoples, the establishment of a judiciary system, and a successful war with Moab and Ammon.

The story of Judah is not resumed until II Kings 8:16.

The Insignificant Reign of Ahaziah in Israel
(I Kings 22:51—II Kings 1:18)

The reader must now be even more on his guard against confusing the historical sequences in Judah and Israel, since kings with the same names—Ahaziah, Jehoram (Joram), and Jehoash (Joash)—appear in both lists, though not in the same order. Only one item significant for secular history is recorded for the brief, two-year reign of Ahaziah of Israel: the revolt of Moab (II Kings 1:1), an event which will be dealt with in considerable detail in 3:4-27. Most of the space allotted to Ahaziah's reign is occupied by a single story from the Elijah cycle, which has to do with the manner of the king's death. The king had suffered severe injuries because of an unexplained fall through the lattice of a second-story window in his palace at Samaria. Instead of consulting the God of Israel, he sent representatives to the shrine of the Philistine god, Baal-zebub, at Ekron, the nearest of the five cities of the Philistines, with instructions to learn from the god's oracle whether or not he would recover. No explanation is given of why he should have resorted to this god rather than to Baal-Melkart, the god of his mother, or any of the other gods in whom the countryside abounded, but presumably Baal-zebub had a reputation for being especially useful in cases of this sort. The name Baal-zebub means literally "the Lord of flies," but it is probably a mocking name, used by the Hebrews for a god called properly Baal-zebul, "Baal the Prince." In later Hebrew religion, this god of the Philistines was degraded to the status of a demon, Be-elzebul, and as such he appears in the Gospels (Matt. 12:27). According to the common theology of the ancient Near East, Ahaziah's action did not necessarily imply disloyalty to the God of Israel. Various gods were useful in different situations; for Ahaziah, no doubt, the Lord's chief concern was with battles and affairs of state. But such an attitude was abhorrent to Elijah and to other adherents of the ancient distinctive religion of Israel, for whom the Lord *alone* was the God of his people and was adequate not merely to meet the needs of the nation in great emergencies but also to deal with every conceivable human situation. So Elijah intercepted the messengers and gave them the Lord's answer to the king's question, whether Ahaziah wished it or not. "The angel of the LORD" who appears in verses 3 and 15 is actually the Lord himself. The phrase is used here, as in some other places in the

Old Testament, to avoid the implication that God appears as man and speaks with a human voice. The Hebrew word translated "angel" means simply messenger and is so translated in verse 2. Verse 8 is interesting because of its mention of the hairy mantle which was the distinctive garb of a prophet (compare I Kings 19:19; Zech. 13:4; Matt. 3:4).

Up to this point our sympathies are thoroughly engaged on Elijah's side, for his insistence on absolute loyalty to God is not only a basic principle of the Bible but is in accord with the best instincts of all high religion. When, however, the story goes on to tell us that Elijah twice called down lightning from heaven to destroy bands of soldiers who were sent to arrest him and who were but the innocent executors of the king's command, we sense an inadequate understanding of God's justice and mercy. If we have any hesitation at passing this kind of judgment on the biblical record, it is reassuring to recall that our Lord's judgment was precisely the same. When two of his disciples proposed to punish some inhospitable Samaritans in identical fashion, Jesus rebuked them (Luke 9:51-55). In some manuscripts the point of his rebuke has been made more explicit by the insertion of the words, "the Son of man came not to destroy men's lives but to save them" (Luke 9:55, see margin). Whether the words are original in this place or not, there can be no doubt that they express accurately Jesus' judgment of the value of human life. It is probably both kinder and more accurate to feel that this particular incident in the biography of Elijah reflects the popular idea of a prophet rather than the behavior or attitude of the prophet himself. This is the only story of the kind told of Elijah.

The Crucial Reign of Jehoram in Israel (2:1—8:15)

When Ahaziah died in accordance with the prophecy of Elijah, the throne descended to his son Jehoram, the fourth and last ruler of the dynasty of Omri. He is also known as Joram, an abbreviated form of the same name (9:14). Jezebel was, of course, still very much alive, and as queen mother she was a powerful figure in the court (compare I Kings 15:13). Just to complete the picture we may note that Jehoram's aunt, Athaliah (Jezebel's daughter), was the wife of King Jehoram of Judah (whose reign was almost exactly contemporary with that of Jehoram of Israel). So in a sense the family of Omri and Ahab was

in control of both kingdoms. Some knowledge of these dynastic
complications is important for understanding the later developments of the story, especially in chapters 9-11.

The Ascension of Elijah (2:1-18)

Once more, after a brief interlude from the editor (1:17-18),
we find ourselves engaged in reading extracts from the collection
of popular tales which told of the experiences of Elijah and
Elisha. Although the first incident is that of Elijah's ascension, the
story is probably to be considered as the beginning of the Elisha
cycle rather than the end of the Elijah, since the center of interest lies in the empowering of Elisha to carry on Elijah's work
through the gift of a double portion of his master's spirit.
In the other Elisha stories, as here, we frequently find the
prophet associated with "the sons of the prophets," communities
of professional men of God, who lived together somewhat on the
order of later communities of monks or dervishes. Elisha was evidently of a much more gregarious temperament than Elijah,
whose solitariness is one of his outstanding traits. In other respects also, as we shall note, Elisha had much in common with
the professional prophets.

The Gilgal mentioned in verse 1 is not the famous shrine of
that name located near Jericho, but one somewhere in the central
hill country of Ephraim above Bethel. From this point Elijah and
Elisha began their last journey together, traveling first to Bethel
and finally down to Jericho in the deep abyss of the Jordan Valley. At each of these stations they met with groups of local prophets, who warned Elisha that his master was about to be taken
from him. But in spite of the entreaties of Elijah, Elisha refused
to be left behind. In full, though distant, view of fifty members of
the prophetic community at Jericho, Elijah struck the waters of
the river with his mantle (compare 1:8); they then separated and
permitted him and his disciple to pass over dry-shod. On the
other side Elijah asked Elisha what gift he wanted above everything else, and Elisha answered that he wished to be recognized
as Elijah's legitimate successor by being given a double portion
of his spirit—that is, the portion which the ordinary law of inheritance allowed to the eldest son (Deut. 21:17). The older
prophet assured his pupil that if he saw him when he was taken
from him it would be a sign that his wish had been granted. The
wish was granted, and he saw Elijah ascend heavenward in a fiery

chariot with a whirlwind. His almost agonized cry, "My father, my father! the chariots of Israel and its horsemen!" means that Israel had suffered a great loss, for Elijah had been to the nation a defense more powerful than horses and chariots. A similar lament would be made one day for Elisha (13:14).

On his return journey Elisha manifested his newly acquired powers by using his master's mantle, now finally fallen upon him (compare I Kings 19:19), to divide the waters of the Jordan as Elijah had done. The prophetic community promptly recognized his authority and paid formal homage to him as Elijah's designated successor. After securing Elisha's reluctant consent, they dispatched a group across the river to see if any harm might have befallen Elijah, but the search proved fruitless and was abandoned at the end of three days. Thus Elijah disappears from the stage of history as suddenly and dramatically as he had once appeared—except that he did not disappear from Israel's memory. The strange manner of his departure, leaving behind him neither grave nor corpse, gave rise to a multitude of legends to the effect that he was still alive and would one day return to complete his work. Such stories have continued to live among orthodox Jews down to the present day. Traces of them are to be found in later parts of the Bible (see Mal. 4:5; Matt. 11:14; 16:14; 27:49; John 1:21). Most striking is Elijah's appearance on the Mount of Transfiguration, as representing the Prophets, along with Moses who represents the Law (Matt. 17:3-4, 10-13).

This chapter is a very interesting one for studying the biblical conception of "spirit." Note especially that "spirit" obviously means "power" and could easily be so translated in verses 9 and 15; notice also that the Hebrew word can mean "wind" and that in verse 16 it could just as well be translated that way, especially when connected with the whirlwind mentioned in verse 11; and, finally, note that "spirit" is a substance which can be measured out (vs. 9). (In John 3:34 it is stated, by contrast, that the Spirit was given to Jesus *without* measure, a sign of his limitless superiority to all the prophets and men of God before him.)

Two Miracles of Elisha (2:19-25)

Further evidence of Elisha's succession to Elijah's powers is provided by the two miracle stories inserted at this point. The first tells of a spring near Jericho whose waters were poisonous and destructive. Elisha "healed" the waters and made them productive. In later tradition this spring was identified with the great spring of Ain es-Sultan, just above the present-day city of Jericho. The second tale is a distinctly unpleasant one about the appalling punishment visited by the prophet on a group of boys who mocked his baldness. It has been suggested, with some plausibility, that the baldness was a kind of tonsure, a sign of Elisha's prophetic office, in which case the boys were being sacrilegious, not merely rude. The modern reader, however, thinking in the light of the New Testament, is likely to pass upon it much the same kind of judgment as we felt impelled to pass on the story in 1:5-12.

A Campaign Against Moab (3:1-27)

The customary editorial formula introducing Jehoram occurs in this chapter (vss. 1-3) rather than in chapter 2, although the end of Elijah's career as related in 2:1-18 obviously took place near the beginning of Jehoram's reign. Jehoram is given the same unfavorable judgment as all the northern kings except for the slight modification in verse 2, which indicates that he had at least a measure of sympathy for the reforming movement of the prophets.

In 1869 a remarkable monument was accidentally discovered near Dhiban (biblical "Dibon"), east of the Dead Sea. It proved to have been set up by Mesha, the Moabite king whose name occurs in verse 4 of chapter 3, and to contain his own story (in a language almost identical with biblical Hebrew) of how the land had been captured by Omri, king of Israel, because of the anger of Chemosh, the chief god of the Moabites. Mesha goes on to say that he himself had at last been able to administer a decisive defeat to Israel and thus win independence for Moab once again. This monument, which is known as the "Moabite" or "Mesha" Stone (now at the Louvre in Paris), is one of the greatest archaeological discoveries of all time and provides interesting confirmation of the situation presupposed by this chapter.

King Mesha is introduced in verse 4 as a "sheep breeder," a word which occurs elsewhere in the Old Testament only in connection with the prophet Amos (Amos 1:1). Although Elisha appears in the course of the narrative, he plays a subordinate role, and it is generally assumed that the section comes from a special source such as that found in I Kings 20 and 22, rather than from the

Elijah-Elisha cycle represented by I Kings 17-19, 21, and II Kings 1:2-17. Mesha's rebellion against Israelite rule is said to have begun during the brief reign of Ahaziah (vs. 5; compare 1:1). In his inscription Mesha himself says that he rebelled in the time of Omri's son. If this were taken literally it would mean that the revolt occurred during the days of Ahab, but the term "son" is used in so general a sense by the Semites that one cannot assume this to be the real meaning of the phrase. The present narrative describes an attempt on the part of Jehoram, assisted by his ally Jehoshaphat of Judah and the king of Edom, to defeat Mesha and reconquer his land. They decided to attack Moab from the south by a circuitous route around the lower end of the Dead Sea, but the campaign nearly came to a calamitous end when they failed to find water at a place where they were sure of it. In the emergency they sought supernatural guidance from the prophet Elisha, who happened to be with the expedition. Despite his antagonism to the royal house of Israel, Elisha was persuaded to help, and he called for a musician to create the mood necessary for inducing a prophetic ecstasy. His use of this artificial device, common among many other people than the Hebrews, shows how much closer Elisha was to the professional prophets than his master Elijah had been. Whereas Elijah seems always to have received the word of God directly and spontaneously, it was "when the minstrel played" that the prophetic trance ("the power of the LORD") came over Elisha. The alleviation promised in verse 17 and fulfilled in verse 20 came through a sudden cloudburst which filled the bed of the stream.

It is said that when the Moabites looked down into the valley under the red rays of the rising sun they mistook the water for blood and imagined that a sanguinary battle had broken out amongst the allies. Made overbold by their error, they incautiously advanced on the enemy and were disastrously routed. The defeat was so overwhelming that the invading armies were able to seize all their land and deliberately ruin it (in violation of the humanitarian law now found in the Book of Deuteronomy; compare vs. 19 with Deut. 20:19-20), except for Mesha's capital city, Kir-hareseth (the modern Kerak). Thus Elisha's prophecy (vs. 18) was fulfilled.

But this was not yet the end of the story. The besieged King Mesha first made a desperate effort to smash through the lines of his attackers, probably in order to join his natural ally, the king of Syria to the north. (Since the Hebrew words for "Edom" and "Syria" are easily confused, the relevant words in verse 26 should most likely be read "to break through to the king of Syria.") Failing even in this, he found refuge in the grim practice of superstition. Like many ancient peoples, including at times even the Hebrews (see, for example, II Kings 16:3 and 21:6), the Moabites believed that of all the sacrifices which could be offered, the sacrifice of one's child—especially the first-born son —was the most perfect and efficacious. Even relatively advanced people, who did not ordinarily practice human sacrifice, might be driven to it in times of stress, when every other recourse seemed to have failed. So Mesha offered his eldest son and designated successor as a whole burnt offering upon the walls of his city, undoubtedly in full sight of the besieging armies. The effect on Israel was catastrophic. The religion of the common man among the Hebrews was not essentially different from that of neighboring countries; the same superstitions were accepted everywhere. So when the soldiers of the allied armies saw the dreadful sacrifice, panic broke out amongst them and they fled back to their own lands. At any rate, this seems the most probable interpretation of the cryptic words with which the chapter concludes. It may appear strange that our Bible could contain a story which seems to confirm belief in the efficacy of human sacrifice—even sacrifice to a heathen god, Chemosh of Moab—but this is another striking bit of evidence of the basic honesty of the Deuteronomic historians and their fidelity in the use of their sources. They have unhesitatingly included this story—told, as it came to them, in terms of popular theology—because they realized its importance for the history of the times.

Elisha and the Widow's Oil (4:1-7)

We now come to a long section (4:1—6:23) which consists entirely of extracts from the popular Elijah-Elisha source. (Elisha is also the hero of the stories in 6:24—8:15, but in most of that section the interest is at least as much in historical and political developments as in the character of Elisha.) These stories are not arranged in any chronological sequence, but are chosen to illustrate various phases of Elisha's wonder-working career. For the most part they tell of deeds of kindness—raising the dead (4: 8-37), healing the sick (ch. 5), multiplying loaves of bread (4:42-44), helping in various emergencies (4:1-7, 38-41; 6:1-7);

in only one instance does Elisha use his powers as an instrument
of national policy (6:8-23). This collection of tales is especially
valuable because it shows us the character of Elisha as reflected
in the popular mind. The number of stories told about him indicates what a tremendous impression he made upon his generation,
partly, of course, because of his success in accomplishing the
task of religious reformation which Elijah had begun but also because he was a kindly and sympathetic person (in spite of 2:
23-25!) who had a reputation for being helpful to people in need.
Two of the stories in this chapter (vss. 1-7 and 8-37) are strikingly similar to stories told about Elijah (compare I Kings 17:
8-24), but on the whole they seem more characteristic of Elisha
than of his more austere and remote predecessor. While most of
the stories found in this section may contain some admixture of
elaboration along with fact, it is better not to try to make any
sharp distinction between what is credible and what is not or to
try to rationalize the miracles, but simply to accept the accounts
for what they are: popular stories told to illustrate the character
of one of the great men of ancient Israel.

The first story reveals to us, incidentally, that the professional
prophets, even though they were associated in communities, might
sometimes be married. One of them had died owing a debt and
his creditor was on the point of selling his two sons into slavery,
as was permitted under Hebrew law (compare Exod. 21:7).
When the man's widow appealed to Elisha for help, the prophet
secured for her a miraculous supply of oil, limited only by the
number of empty vessels she had collected and entirely adequate
to pay her husband's debt.

Elisha and the Shunammite Woman's Son (4:8-37)

When on his travels about the country, Elisha was frequently
the guest of a wealthy woman in Shunem (see the comment on
I Kings 1:3), who had set aside for his exclusive use a small
furnished room on the roof of her house. Touched by her generous hospitality, Elisha on one of his visits asked what he could
do to reward her, suggesting that in view of his contacts in high
places he might be able to obtain some special favor from the
civil or military authorities. She, however, reminded him that
she was a woman of high social position herself and had no need
of the special intercession of others. In fact, she refused to ask
for any gift at all. At this point we meet for the first time Elisha's

personal servant, Gehazi, who evidently performed the same services for him that he himself had previously performed for Elijah
(3:11). Gehazi reminded the prophet that his hostess was child-
less and that her husband was so old as to make it unlikely that
she ever would have children in the natural way. Since childless-
ness was the greatest of misfortunes for a Hebrew woman, Elisha
could certainly do her no finer service than to remedy this defect,
so he drew upon his prophetic powers and announced that she
would become the mother of a son after the lapse of the usual
time of pregnancy (which is apparently the meaning of the
phrase, "when the time comes round," in verse 16). Although
she expressed a quite natural skepticism about it, the passing
months fully justified the prophet's promise, and in due time she
bore a son.

The story then leaps over a number of years to a period when
the boy was old enough to go out into the field and watch the
harvesters. The hot Palestinian sun proved too much for him, as
it has for many others, and the story vividly pictures the child's
pathetic cries as he falls with a fatal sunstroke. From the verses
which follow (vss. 22-25) we learn, incidentally, that it was a
common custom to pay visits to holy men at the new moon and on
the Sabbath (the husband thinks it strange that his wife should
go at any other time). We also learn that the prophet made his
headquarters at Mount Carmel, where Elijah had once defeated
the prophets of Baal (I Kings 18:20-46). Anxious to reach Elisha
as quickly as possible with the news of her son's death, the an-
guished mother took a slave to run beside her donkey and beat
him all the twenty-five miles from Shunem to Carmel. Her meeting with the prophet provides the teller of the story with another
fine dramatic scene. Elisha, whose clairvoyant powers were obviously not a permanent possession, was puzzled by her visit at
so unusual a time, but he could see that she was in deep trouble,
and he rebuked Gehazi for treating her with the insensitivity
which seems to have been a mark of his character (compare
5:19b-27). Just the mention of the boy by the woman was sufficient to reveal the true situation to the prophet, who immediately sent Gehazi to her house with his wonder-working staff in
hand and a blessing on his lips, which Elisha ordered him not to
dissipate by idle greetings on the way. But in response to the
mother's insistence, Elisha went himself, and the staff having
proved to be of no avail, he breathed his own breath into the

still body of the child. The story comes to a moving end as the mother happily carries her son, once dead but now alive again, from the prophet's little room.

A further incident involving this woman is related in 8:1-6.

Elisha and the Poisoned Stew (4:38-41)

On one of his visits to the prophetic community at Gilgal near Jericho, during a time of famine (perhaps the one mentioned in 8:1), Elisha was able to use his wonderful powers to counteract the deadly properties of a poisonous wild vegetable which had by accident been mixed with edible plants in the common dish.

Elisha Feeds a Multitude (4:42-44)

On another occasion a devotee brought a special gift of fresh grain and twenty loaves of bread made from the first ears of barley harvested in his field. The offering of the "first fruits" for religious purposes was an ancient custom in Israel as elsewhere (Exod. 23:19). When Elisha ordered that the gift be used for feeding the entire prophetic community, consisting of a hundred men, Gehazi characteristically interposed the practical objection that the amount was insufficient, but the prophet's judgment proved correct, for marvelously there was enough and to spare. The similarity between this story and those of our Lord's feeding of the multitude (Mark 6:30-44; 8:1-9) has often been noted.

Elisha Heals a Leper from Syria (5:1-27)

Periods of peace alternated with periods of war in the long struggle between Israel and the neighbor kingdom of Syria, fought chiefly over possession of the disputed territories in northern Transjordan. The incident with which the present chapter is concerned must have occurred in one of the interludes of peace, but it cannot be dated more precisely since the names of the two kings are not given and no attempt is made to relate it to the general history of the times. From the opening verse it would seem that the fortunes of war had recently turned in Syria's favor. It is interesting to note that an Israelite writer attributes the Syrian victory to "the LORD," the God of his own people, just as Mesha had explained Omri's victory over Moab in terms of the anger of Chemosh (see the comment on 3:1-27). In both instances a national god is recognized as having supranational power. In Israel, and in Israel alone, the full implications of this idea were developed to their logical conclusion, so that the God of Israel came to be conceived of as a universal God sitting in judgment upon *all* nations and ruling the world in accord with his righteous and immutable law (see, for example, Isa. 45:20-24). The ideas found in verse 1 are not so advanced as that, but the germinal thought—that the Lord is the giver of victory to Syrians as well as to Israelites—is there (compare also vs. 15). Its further development is the contribution of the great prophets.

Naaman, the commander-in-chief of the Syrian armies, is described as a victim of leprosy, but the biblical term is a general one covering a variety of skin diseases, so it does not necessarily mean that he had the affliction now called by that name. (In Leviticus 14:34-47 the word is used for some kind of mold on the house wall!) Fortunately for Naaman, there was a little Israelite slave girl in his household, who had been captured by a raiding party and sold to his wife as a personal maid; she felt sorry for him and told her mistress of the remarkable therapeutic powers of the prophet Elisha. So Naaman applied to his royal master for permission to visit Israel and consult the prophet. He received both the necessary permission and a letter of recommendation to the Israelite king. A note of humor is injected into the story by a misunderstanding on the part of the king of Israel, who jumped to the unsettling conclusion that his brother king in Syria, perhaps his suzerain at this time, was trying to provoke a quarrel by asking him to do the impossible. His peace of mind was no doubt restored when Elisha, having heard the story, came forward to offer his services. A further bit of humor is provided by Naaman's reaction to the prophet's casual and, to his mind, undignified treatment of him. He confesses that he had expected the prophet to come out and greet him personally and then heal him with solemn prayers and dramatic gestures. But, instead, Elisha did not even talk with him, but merely sent a servant with the message that he should bathe seven times in the Jordan River. The great nobleman's anger at such uncivil treatment found expression in a contemptuous comparison of the Jordan with the far finer rivers of Damascus. If what he had needed was a bath, he could have had a better one at home! In a sense the point was well taken, for the beautiful rivers of Damascus make possible the fertile oasis—one of the garden spots of the world—on which that city is built. The Jordan, on the other hand, is an unimpressive stream which flows for miles in its deeply eroded channel through an almost barren waste before finally dumping its waters in the sterile depths of the Dead Sea. But underneath the surface humor of the tale there is a serious lesson which Naaman's servants are not slow to point out to their master. It is really a twofold lesson: first, that God can work just as effectively through little things as through big (a frequent biblical theme); and, second, that what he requires above all else is simple obedience to his commands. When Naaman is induced at last, reluctantly, to test the prescription of the prophet, he emerges from the water with flesh as clean as that of a little child.

The sequel tells of Naaman's confession of the glory and power of the Lord and his resolve henceforth to worship him alone. Nevertheless he asked the prophet for two concessions, both of which were granted: first, that he might be permitted to carry back to Damascus some of the soil of Israel so that he might literally worship the Lord on the Lord's own land; and, second, that when he joined officially in the worship of the royal Syrian court, an obligation he could hardly avoid, he might be forgiven if for the sake of appearances he prostrated himself before Rimmon, the god of his master and his people. The first of these items illustrates how literally the people of the ancient Near East took the idea that any god was only the god of a particular territory (compare I Kings 20:23; II Kings 17:26; I Sam. 26:19); the second item has provided us with a proverbial saying, "To bow down in the house of Rimmon," meaning to conform, for reasons of policy, to some reprehensible custom. At the end of the chapter the detestable Gehazi takes the center of the stage. When Elisha refused the gift which Naaman had proffered, Gehazi despised him for the act and thought he saw an opportunity to gain some advantage for himself. So, having hastily contrived a story about some newly arrived visitors, he went after Naaman and asked for a generous present to be given them. Naaman gladly acceded to the request, but Gehazi had failed to take account of Elisha's miraculous powers of second sight. On his return, Elisha accused him of his crime and, by way of punishment, caused him—and his descendants after him—to be infected with the leprosy of Naaman. The story ends on a note of most solemn warning as the greedy Gehazi, who only a few moments before had thought himself to be both clever and rich, goes out the door "a leper, as white as snow."

Elisha and the Floating Axhead (6:1-7)

This is the most trivial of the stories told of Elisha, but it is interesting as an illustration of the prophet's willingness to be helpful even in small matters. The prophetic community over which Elisha presided had grown so large that it was necessary to seek for larger quarters. In the course of erecting a new building near the Jordan River one of the men lost a borrowed axhead in the water, but Elisha used his supernatural powers and recovered it for him.

Elisha Captures a Band of Syrian Soldiers (6:8-23)

Once again we find ourselves in the context of the Syrian wars, but the major interest in this story is with Elisha himself and no clue is given as to the relationship of the episode to the general course of the conflict. Both kings in the story are anonymous, and the locale of the opening scene is left deliberately vague. Elisha's clairvoyant gifts have made it possible for him on a number of occasions to reveal to his master, the king of Israel, the movements of the Syrian forces and thus enable him to avoid entanglement with them. Perplexed by the consistent failure of his well-laid plans, the Syrian king suspected the presence of a spy within his own ranks, but at length he was informed that Elisha was responsible. He determined to seize the prophet at the first opportunity, and learning that Elisha was temporarily in Dothan, about ten miles north of Samaria, the king sent a considerable body of men, at night, to surround the city and arrest him. That the Syrians were able to approach with impunity so close to the Hebrew capital is, of course, an indication of the great weakness of Israel at this stage of the war. When, in the morning, Elisha's servant (Gehazi?) discovered the presence of the enemy army, he was naturally terrified and could imagine no possible way of escape. It was then that Elisha gave utterance to one of the great texts of the Books of Kings: "Fear not, for those who are with us are more than those who are with them" (vs. 16). This is the kind of faith which had sustained the men of Israel from the very beginning of their history (compare, for example, Judges 5:20) and would become one of the foundation stones of later prophetic teaching (compare Isa. 31:1-9; 37:33-35; 40:21-31; Zech. 4:6; Matt. 26:53). The issue of battles is not determined by the largest battalions, but by him who is called "the LORD of hosts," who has all the powers of the universe at his command. When Elisha prayed that the grounds of his own confidence might be visibly revealed to his disciple, the latter's eyes were opened to see the mountains round about "full of horses and chariots of fire." Then, at Elisha's instance, the enemy soldiers were miraculously blinded so that he was able to lead them to Samaria and deliver them into the hand of the king of Israel.

It is fortunate that the story does not end at this point, for one might be inclined to blame Elisha for using his supernatural powers (none too scrupulously, judging by verse 19) for purely nationalistic ends. The conclusion, however, shows the prophet in a most generous and kindly mood, rebuking the king for even the thought of killing the prisoners he had taken in so remarkable a fashion and ordering that instead they be fed and set free.

Elisha at the Siege of Samaria (6:24—7:20)

This story, like the preceding one of Elisha's adventure at Dothan (6:8-23), has to do with the Syrian war but differs from that story in its greater concern for actual history. Some interpreters assign it to the source represented by I Kings 20 and 22 rather than to the collection of popular tales about Elijah and Elisha from which most of this group is taken. Although the king of Syria is identified as Ben-hadad, the information is not so useful as it might be, since more than one Syrian ruler bore this name (compare 8:7-15 with 13:3). Unhappily, the Israelite king is not identified at all and has been variously conjectured to be either Jehoram, as the present position of the story would suggest, or a later king, Jehoahaz (13:1-9; note especially 13:3).

Although the last sentence of 6:23 states that guerilla bands from Syria no longer dared to roam freely in Israel, the war was by no means at an end, and verse 24 tells of a full-scale invasion by Ben-hadad which resulted in a blockade of the capital city. The purpose of a siege is, of course, to starve a city into surrender by cutting off its supplies of food. The effectiveness of this particular siege is demonstrated by the fabulous prices which were being paid in Samaria for the most contemptible and repulsive articles of diet. But more appalling than that was the resort to cannibalism, a practice well attested elsewhere in the Bible under similar circumstances (Lam. 4:10). Confronted with evidence of such abominations, the king, whose sincere though unostentatious piety was revealed by the sackcloth he wore beneath his garments, swore to destroy Elisha, who had apparently encouraged the king to resist in hope of a divine intervention. Through his supernatural prescience the prophet knew of the king's threat and refused to admit his messenger, certain that the king himself would be coming immediately behind him. On the arrival of the king, Elisha assured him that the famine was almost over and that the next day would see the resumption of a more normal food supply. When the king's military aide rather rudely expressed some doubts about the accuracy of the prophet's information, Elisha with equal acerbity responded that though the officer would witness the fulfillment of the promise he would, as punishment for his skepticism, derive no personal benefit from the fact.

That evening four lepers, despairing of their lot, decided to desert to the enemy; after all, the Syrians could do no more than kill them, and if they stayed they would die anyway! To their amazement, however, when they reached the besiegers' camp they found it empty, for the Lord had infected the Syrian army with panic, causing them to hear a sound like that of a great approaching army. A rumor had spread among them that the king of Israel had succeeded in hiring allies from the Hittites and Egyptians, whose forces were now at hand. The ensuing flight had taken place with such speed and disorder that the tents, the baggage, and even the animals were left behind. Gleefully the lepers began to plunder the camp, but finally they remembered their responsibility toward the starving city which they had forsaken. Motivated by fear of punishment as much as by a sense of duty, they notified the gatekeepers of what they had found, and these in turn sent word to the king. Quite naturally he found the story difficult to believe and suspected a ruse on the part of the Syrians. But a small searching party which was sent out quickly confirmed the lepers' story and was able to track the panic-stricken Syrian army all the way to the Jordan River by the clothes and implements they had dropped in their flight.

As soon as the word was spread among the citizens of Samaria, they rushed out through the city gate in a mob to plunder the deserted camp. This scene provides the necessary background for the last incident in the story, the punishment of the king's aide for his skeptical reaction to Elisha's prophecy. He was the man to whom the king had given charge of the gate, and when the

starved and greedy populace came tearing out of the city, he fell
down before them and was crushed to death. Once again we feel
ourselves in the presence of a spirit which seems out of harmony
with what we know of the prophet's kindliness and generosity as
exemplified in some of the other stories (compare 6:21-23).
Such inconsistencies may, of course, have been genuinely present
in the character of Elisha, and we must be careful not to modern-
ize, Christianize, or sentimentalize these figures from a world so
far away in time and so different from our own. There can, however, be no doubt that ferocity had a special appeal for tellers
of popular tales. No one can mistake the relish with which the
ancient storyteller dwells upon this gruesome incident, twice repeating the dreadful phrase, "the people trod upon him in the gate,
so that he died" (vss. 17, 20). The message which the story is designed to convey—that of the need for simple trust in the promises of God—is one which needs to be heard, even if for Christian ears the manner of the telling leaves something to be desired.

Elisha Helps the Shunammite Woman Again (8:1-6)

Elisha's remarkable insight having made it possible for him to
predict the coming of a long famine in Israel, he warned his good
friend the Shunammite woman, whose son he had restored to life
(4:8-37), that she would be well advised to migrate temporarily
to a foreign country, so she spent the whole period of seven years
in the land of the Philistines. On her return to Israel she discovered that she had forfeited her property in the interim and so
went to present a petition to the king for its restitution. As good
fortune would have it, Elisha's servant Gehazi happened to be at
court just at that moment, telling the king some stories of Elisha's
wonderful deeds and especially how he had brought the dead to
life. The woman's petition was given a particular interest in the
king's eyes when Gehazi was able to point out that she and her
son were the ones of whom he just had been speaking. As a consequence the king promptly ordered the restoration of her property with all the income which she had lost and sent an officer
with her to see that his orders were carried out. It will be recalled
that Elisha had offered previously to use his influence at court
on her behalf (4:13); the present story shows that the offer had
not been an idle one. This fact, added to the statement in 3:2, indicates that Jehoram's relation to the prophetic movement was
more sympathetic than the subsequent course of events would

seem to indicate. Small apparent discrepancies of this kind are interesting as evidence that the history of the monarchy and the characters involved in it was a good deal more complicated than the hasty reader of these books might suppose.

Elisha's Meeting with Hazael (8:7-15)

Once more (as in 6:24—7:20) we find Elisha involved in matters of great historical importance rather than simply playing the role of the popular wonder-worker and friend of people in need. This time, however, the subject is not his influence upon political events in Israel, but, remarkably enough, his intrusion into the affairs of Israel's chief enemy, Syria. The next chapter deals with the way in which Elisha instigated a revolt against the reigning dynasty in Israel; here we find him performing a similar function among the Syrians. In both instances the narrative regards him as obeying the divine command given to Elijah at Horeb (I Kings 19:15-17).

Learning that the prophet was paying a visit to Damascus, the sick king, Ben-hadad, sent an official of his court, a certain Hazael, with gifts to find out from Elisha whether or not he would recover. The prophet indulged himself in the privilege, often used in ancient oracles, of speaking ambiguously. The official reply was that the king would recover (speaking, presumably, with reference only to the probable course of his illness); but a private message, spoken secretly to Hazael, informs him that the king is doomed to die. Whether this should be considered an invitation to murder is a delicate question, depending on one's point of view. To Elisha, no doubt, it was simply an announcement of an event which he saw already determined by the Lord; to Hazael, on the other hand, it was a subtle suggestion which he immediately planned to follow. That Elisha took no pleasure in his fateful prophecy is indicated by the horror which overcame him as he beheld in his mind's eye the deeds of frightfulness which Hazael and his troops would one day perform in the land of Israel (for the fulfillment of the vision see 10:32-33 and Amos 1:3-5). Hazael's comment, "What is your servant, who is but a dog . . . ?", was not spoken as an echo of Elisha's horror, but as a formal act of modesty and self-depreciation in view of the high destiny to which the prophet seemed to be summoning him. This humility was thoroughly in character, since Hazael was a man of such humble origins that the record does not even give us the name

of his father, and a contemporary Assyrian inscription describes
him as "son of a nobody." Nevertheless, he had no hesitation in
returning to the palace and smothering his master, after which he
seized the throne for himself.

The Reign of Jehoram in Judah (8:16-24)

Contrary to his usual rule, the historian here interrupts his account of Jehoram's reign in Israel to bring his readers up to date
on events in Judah, a procedure made necessary by the close interweaving of the history of the two kingdoms in the chapters
which immediately follow. During the long middle part of the
reign of Jehoram of Israel (in vs. 16 called Joram, but compare
3:1), the king of Judah was a brother-in-law of the same name,
husband of the infamous Athaliah. According to the Chronicler,
this Jehoram, in typical despotic fashion, had all his brothers
murdered when he ascended the throne (II Chron. 21:4). The
Deuteronomic historian is undoubtedly right in saying that the
policies of Judah and Israel were identical at this period (vs. 18).
The chief political events recorded of the reign of Jehoram of
Judah are the revolt of Edom (vs. 20), which had been under
Judean domination during Jehoshaphat's time (I Kings 22:47;
II Kings 3:9), and that of Libnah, a city southwest of Jerusalem
on the edge of the coastal plain (vs. 22). In the case of Edom, in
spite of a certain and possibly intentional vagueness in the narrative, Jehoram (now called Joram, vs. 21) seems to have barely
escaped complete disaster by breaking through encircling enemy
forces. The Chronicler adds some information about a successful
foray made upon Judah by the Philistines and Arabs (II Chron.
21:16-17), and reports that Jehoram died of an agonizing disease
in accordance with a prophecy of Elijah (II Chron. 21:11-15,
18-19).

The Reign of Ahaziah in Judah (8:25-29)

The reason for the interpolation of the account of the two
Judean kings, Jehoram and Ahaziah, becomes evident in this passage, where the historian explains how Ahaziah, whose reign
lasted less than a year, happened to be in the company of Jehoram of Israel on the occasion when both of them were assassinated (9:21-29). Like Ahab and Jehoshaphat before them (I

Kings 22:1-36), Jehoram of Israel and Ahaziah of Judah had determined on an attempt to recapture the city of Ramoth-gilead in northern Transjordan, which was still in the hands of the Syrian king, the usurper Hazael. Jehoram (Joram) was wounded during one of the battles and had returned to the royal estate at Jezreel to recuperate, where, when the narrative in chapter 8 breaks off, he is enjoying a friendly visit from Ahaziah. The Deuteronomic historian never bothers to bring his account of Ahaziah's reign to a formal close, but the essential information is all contained in the following chapter in the story of Jehoram's fall (9:21-29). The thread of official Judean history is resumed only at 11:1.

The Revolution of Jehu (9:1—10:28)

After the brief interlude of Judean history, the editor returns to the story of events in Israel, which were rapidly coming to a crisis. The conflict between the dynasty of Omri, with its international connections and syncretistic religious policies, and the conservative devotees of the ancient religion, which had been smoldering ever since Ahab's accession to the throne, was now about to break out into a flame of revolt which would consume the royal house and all its works. The architect of the revolt was Elisha, intent upon completing the program assigned to his master Elijah (I Kings 19:16). He appears, however, only in the opening scene, the rest of the story being told with Jehu in the center of the stage.

While the armies of Israel were encamped on the field of Ramoth-gilead and the two kings were momentarily away from their commands because of Jehoram's injury, Elisha commissioned a member of the prophetic community to go to Jehu—a commander of the Israelite forces who was evidently well known for his devotion to the ideals of the prophetic party as well as for his ambitious and violent nature—and solemnly anoint him as king to reign in Jehoram's stead. Arrived at the camp, the messenger called Jehu out from the council of officers and secretly performed the ceremony of anointing. His fellow officers were naturally curious at the meaning of the sudden interruption, but when informed of its purpose, they rallied immediately to Jehu's side and publicly proclaimed him king. It is interesting to notice the popular evaluation of a prophet in the partly contemptuous phrase "this mad fellow" (vs. 11). One must say *partly* contemptuous, because to the ancient mind madness was also regarded with awe as a sign of divine possession, and the mood of frenzy was for this reason regularly cultivated by the professional prophets (I Sam. 10:5-6, 10; I Kings 18:28-29). The common worldly man in every age tends to view the religious enthusiast in this ambivalent way—with emotions compounded of sincere respect tinctured, if ever so slightly, with aversion and contempt.

The scenes which follow are among the most dramatic in the Bible. Jehu, immediately on receiving the acclamation of his brother officers, leaped into his chariot and drove off full speed for Jezreel at the head of a considerable number of his soldiers, anxious to forestall any effort to bring warning of the revolt to the two kings who were at their ease on the royal estate. From the watchtower at Jezreel a sentinel saw him coming in the distance and reported to Jehoram that an unidentified body of troops was rapidly approaching. The king promptly ordered an officer to go out and meet them and find out why they were there. No sooner had the officer arrived than, at Jehu's invitation, he joined the rebels. The sentinel on his tower reported the messenger's failure to return, so a second was sent, with the same result. This time, of course, the band was much closer and the watchman was able to identify the lead figure as Jehu because of his impetuous driving. The third time it was the king himself, still uncertain of the meaning of these strange events, who went out in his chariot, accompanied by Ahaziah in another, to meet the advancing troops. Jehu lost no time in making clear the purpose of his visit, although it is interesting to note that he expressed no personal enmity toward Jehoram but put the blame entirely upon Jezebel, the queen mother. When the two kings turned to flee, Jehu unhesitatingly drew his bow and sent an arrow straight through the heart of Jehoram. His body, we are told, was left to lie in what had once been Naboth's vineyard, thus fulfilling the prophecy of Elijah (I Kings 21:19-24). Although Ahaziah escaped in the confusion of the moment, the rebels followed and killed him only a few miles away. His body was then carried to Jerusalem by Judean soldiers and given royal burial. In a sense he was an innocent victim of events in which he had no direct concern, but it must not be forgotten that, as Jezebel's grandson, he was an object of the hatred felt in Israel for all the members of the family of Omri.

Since the revolt was really directed against the continuing influence of Jezebel, there could be no rest until she also was destroyed. Nowhere does the strength of Jezebel's character show
more clearly than in the narrative of her death (vss. 30-37). She
was a ruthless woman who could not be terrified by ruthlessness
in others. She had lived like a queen and she died like one. When
she learned that her assassin was at hand, she prepared to receive
him as though at a royal audience, using cosmetics and putting
on her queenly regalia. Far from cringing before Jehu, she
leaned from the palace window and called him "murderer." (For
the reference to Zimri, see I Kings 16:9-10.) Jehu did not deign
to answer but ordered the servants to throw her down into the
courtyard, where she was crushed to death beneath the wheels
of his chariot and the hooves of his horses. Contemptuously leaving her corpse to be mangled by scavenger dogs, the victorious
leader of the revolt proceeded into the palace to refresh himself
with food and drink. When, later, he relented to the extent of
authorizing a queenly burial for her, hardly enough of the body
could be found to identify it as hers. This, too, says the writer,
was in accordance with the prophecy of Elijah (vss. 36-37).

The climactic events described in chapter 9 took place on the
royal estate at Jezreel; it still remained for Jehu to finish his job
in the capital city of Samaria. This is the subject of 10:1-28. He
first of all sent a letter to the guardians of the royal family in
Samaria challenging them to choose another member of the ruling house to be king and let him fight it out with the rebels. But
the news of Jehu's initial success at Jezreel and the trail of royal
blood he had left behind him was enough to discourage any
thought of further resistance. The civil guardians of the palace
at Samaria sent back a fawning reply, asking for instructions
from their new master. He tested their sincerity by ordering them
to massacre all the male descendants of Ahab and send their
heads to Jezreel. They showed no reluctance to do this and sent
the baskets, filled with severed heads (the "seventy" is just a
round number), to the gate of Jezreel. There, evidently at night,
Jehu ordered them to be deposited. In the morning he came out
with the citizens of Jezreel and, feigning surprise, apparently
explained the presence of the two piles of heads as an act of God.
He exonerated the people of the city and, although he readily
admitted his murder of the kings, disclaimed all knowledge of
the heads and how they came to be there. Once again, the teller

of the story refers us to the prophecy of Elijah and underlines
the fact that now the family of Ahab was utterly destroyed
(vs. 10). The elimination of all the members of the old ruling
house was, of course, a necessity for the secure establishment of
the new regime in Israel. No one must be left who could avenge
his kinsmen or make a legitimate claim upon the throne.

Now Jehu might make the trip to Samaria to consolidate his
victory and begin his reign as king. On the way he chanced to
meet a party of princely visitors from Judah who were in Israel
to pay a visit of courtesy on their kinsmen, the members of the
former royal family (vss. 12-14). The reader will not be surprised to learn that they met no kinder fate at Jehu's hands than
did any of the other friends of Jehoram and the queen mother.
The other incident of the journey to Samaria (vss. 15-16) is interesting because it introduces us to Jehonadab the son of Rechab,
the founder of an ultraconservative group or sect in Israel which
more than two centuries later was to figure in a well-known incident in the Book of Jeremiah (Jer. 35:1-19). The members of
this group were so conservative in their devotion to the ancient
religion and so consistent in their opposition to the agricultural
religion and fertility gods of Canaan that they refused to drink
wine (the characteristic product of Canaan), plant fields, or even
live in houses (Jer. 35:6-7). They would naturally be antagonistic to the old ruling house and favorable toward any reform, so
their leader Jehonadab, on meeting Jehu, gladly joined his entourage.

Since Jehu was now in firm possession of the reins of power,
there was no reason to delay the religious reformation which had
been so long desired and which he had been selected to bring
about. However much we may believe his personal motives in
leading the revolt to have been chiefly selfish and secular, there
is no reason to doubt his genuine devotion to the sturdy old national creed of Israel and his antipathy to the debased and form-
less religion with which Ahab and Jezebel proposed to contami-
nate it. Up to this point Jehu had not spared to use deceit and
wholesale murder for the furtherance of his ends, and there would
be no reason to expect him to do so now. The last act of his revolt is perhaps the most sickening of all (vss. 18-28). Professing
an earnest desire to join in the royal cult and summoning all the
worshipers of Baal-Melkart to the temple which Ahab had built
in honor of Jezebel's god (I Kings 16:32), Jehu, assisted by

Jehonadab, set guards at all the gates and ordered the congregation to be slaughtered to a man. The modern reader will inevitably be reminded of the massacre of St. Bartholomew's Eve many
centuries later. When all the worshipers of Baal were dead, the
temple and the material objects of the cult were then destroyed,
and the temple site was converted into a public privy (vss. 26-27).

Reading the history of this revolt, the Christian reader is likely
to be torn by conflicting emotions—fascination at a story of exciting events well told, relief that what was undoubtedly the right
side was victorious, and abhorrence at the uninhibited use of
duplicity and murder in a supposedly righteous cause. First of
all, it needs to be emphasized that there can be no doubt that
the right side won. Jehu himself is quite as ugly a figure as Jezebel, but the principles he stood for were, perhaps accidentally so
far as he was concerned, the only principles which could endure.
The religion which Jezebel represented had no backbone, no real
understanding of either God or man, and was almost entirely de-
ficient in morality. It had nothing new to offer the world and
bore no promise for the future. The ancient religion of Israel,
on the other hand, was virile, profound in its view of God and of
the weaknesses and possibilities of man, and had within it the
germ of a universal morality. For the Christian, of course, it is
also seen to be a part of God's ongoing revelation of himself to
the world, a treasure which needed at all costs to be preserved
for future generations, a stalwart foundation on which one day
the religion of the New Covenant would be built. No excuse can
be offered for the crimes of Jehu, and one cannot suppose that
God willed them; nevertheless we can be grateful that the truth
of God prevailed and that God showed here as in so many other
instances his capacity to turn even "the wrath of men" to his
praise (Ps. 76:10). Finally, if one is tempted to think that these
bloody deeds represent the characteristic temper of Old Testament religion, it is important to realize that just a hundred years
later the prophet Hosea condemned the house of Jehu for the
abominable means by which it had come to power and predicted
for it the same doom that had once been pronounced on the
house of Ahab (Hosea 1:4).

The Unsatisfactory Reign of Jehu in Israel (10:29-36)

The modern reader, who is apt to pass a rather unfavorable
judgment upon the character of Jehu, may be encouraged by the

fact that the Deuteronomic editors of Kings have no enthusiasm for him either. For the account of his revolt they simply reproduce an older document to whose authors Jehu was evidently something of a hero. But when the editors of our book come to tell the story of Jehu's *reign,* they summarize it in their own characteristic language and have nothing good to say of him beyond the fact that he had been successful in wiping out the influence of Ahab and his family. While syncretism in the crude form of Jezebel's attempt to introduce the worship of Baal-Melkart had been decisively rejected, the more subtle form which had long endangered the purity of religion in Israel remained untouched. Jehu made no effort to eliminate the bull-images at Dan and Bethel and presumably did nothing to counteract the tendency to confuse the character of the God of Israel with that of the old fertility gods of the Canaanites. Furthermore, from the political point of view he was a poor ruler. The power of Israel over against Syria under the new and vigorous King Hazael continued to decline until finally all the territory in Transjordan was lost (vss. 32-33). From evidence outside the Bible the weakness of Israel seems due, at least in part, to Jehu's ill-advised alliance with the Assyrians against Hazael. A famous Assyrian monument, the black obelisk of Shalmaneser III, pictures Jehu paying tribute to the Assyrian king; unfortunately for Jehu, Assyria herself was just entering temporarily upon a period of declining influence in the West and was able to give him little support. Although Jehu ruled for 28 years and established a dynasty which lasted through the four following generations (Jehoahaz, Jehoash, Jeroboam II, and Zechariah), his reign, from every point of view except the religious, seems to have been a calamity for Israel.

Since the editors must now go back to tell what happened in Judah after the death of Ahaziah, the history of Israel is interrupted; it continues in chapter 13.

The Evil Reign of Athaliah in Judah (11:1-21)

Jezebel's daughter, Athaliah, the wife of Jehoram of Judah and mother of Ahaziah, was a woman cut from the same strip of cloth as her mother, strong-minded and ruthless in the pursuit of power. When she heard of the revolt in Israel and the death of Ahaziah (9:27-28), it was evident to her that her authority as

queen mother in Judah was mortally threatened, especially because the continuing loyalty of the people of the Southern Kingdom to the Davidic dynasty provided the religion of Yahweh
with a firmer basis of support than it had in the north. So she
immediately took the practical step of ordering the death of all
members of the royal family who might lay claim to the throne.
But the machinations of one woman were thwarted by the quick
thinking of another. Jehosheba, a daughter of Jehoram (Joram)
and, according to the Chronicler (II Chron. 22:11), wife of the
priest Jehoiada, was able to save Joash (Jehoash), an infant son
of Ahaziah, and hide him away for six years in her apartment in
the Temple buildings. When at length a propitious moment came,
Jehoiada, her husband, made preparations for the revolt. The
military orders and operations described in verses 4-11 are not
very clear, but apparently the normal Sabbath arrangements for
the guards of the Temple and the palace were changed so that a
much larger group was on duty in the Temple than was usual.
The captains of the guards first swore secret allegiance to the
young prince (vs. 4), and then the guards protected him while
he was publicly crowned and anointed king of Judah (vs. 12).
It was the shout of "Long live the king!" which first apprised
Athaliah that revolt had broken out. She rushed from the palace,
which of course adjoined the Temple, to cry, "Treason! Treason!", but it was too late. Jehoiada ordered her to be seized and
executed, although from motives of reverence the sentence was
carried out in the royal palace rather than in the Temple.

The religious and constitutional character of the monarchy
was restored when the young king entered into covenants with
the Lord and with the people (vs. 17; compare II Sam. 5:3,
where David also enters into a covenant). The covenant with
God was a reaffirmation of the principle that Israel is the People
of the Lord, the king is his servant, and the Lord alone is to be
recognized as God in Israel. The covenant was a formal rejection
of the attempt to introduce Baal-Melkart, the god of Athaliah,
or any other foreign god into a pantheon in Israel, and it was immediately given practical force by the destruction of Baal's temple
and the execution of his priest. The last act in the ceremony was
a procession, composed of military units and representatives of
the populace, which accompanied the new king to the royal palace and there formally installed him on the throne of his ancestors. The "Carites" in verses 4 and 19 were foreign mercenaries.

The revolution in Judah was a more sober affair than the bloody revolt in Israel. There was evidently none of that admixture of personal ambition which tended to corrupt the good that Jehu undeniably accomplished. It is interesting to note, incidentally, that whereas the prime movers of the revolt in Israel were found amongst the ecstatic prophets, the reforming movement in Judah was organized by a priest. These facts point to certain characteristic differences between the two kingdoms which are not without significance for their later history and the subsequent fate of their respective peoples.

The Reign of Jehoash in Judah (12:1-21)

Since he was only seven when he ascended the throne (11: 21), it is not surprising to learn that Jehoash (also called Joash) reigned for forty years. He would no doubt have reigned much longer had he not been cut down prematurely by assassins. He was raised in the home of a reforming priest who was directly responsible for putting him in power and who for a long time continued as his adviser. Jehoash's reign, therefore, is accounted a good one by the Deuteronomic editors, whose only qualification is the usual one that he did not abolish the "high places," meaning merely that his reform was not as radical as the later one of Josiah, the ideal king of the Deuteronomists.

The story of Jehoash's reign well illustrates the predominantly religious interests of the Deuteronomists, since of all the things that must have happened the only two they chose to relate both have to do with the Temple. The first item is a long account of the measures Jehoash took for repairing the Temple building, which had evidently fallen into a dilapidated state since King Solomon's golden days (vss. 4-16). Jehoash first gave orders that the priests should pay for repairing it out of the income which they received from religious taxes and free will offerings rather than wait for some special grant from the royal treasury. Just when this order was given is not indicated, but, although the priests had agreed to the king's order, by the twenty-third year of his reign they had done nothing to implement it. Jehoash then resolved upon a drastic measure; he ordered that the priests should no longer receive any money from the hands of the people, but that it should all be contributed directly to a restoration fund. In order to carry out the king's plan as efficiently as possible, the priest Jehoiada devised a collection box with a hole in the lid, into which the doorkeepers placed all the offerings that were brought. When a sufficiently large amount had been collected, the chief priest and an official of the court counted it and paid it immediately into the hands of the men who were at work repairing the Temple. It is stated specifically that none of the money was used for the purchase of appurtenances of worship. The impression one gets of Jehoash from this story is that of a strong and able administrator whose chief concern was order and efficiency. The priests were not left entirely devoid of income, since they were allowed to keep for themselves the fines which had to be paid in connection with the guilt offerings and the sin offerings (vs. 16; see Lev. 4:1—6:7 for the law governing these sacrifices).

The second item related of Jehoash's reign is his helplessness before an invasion by Hazael, the king of Syria (vss. 17-18). When even Israel, under Jehu, could not withstand the armies of Syria (10:32-33), it is not surprising that Judah should have been helpless also. Syrian forces penetrated as far as Gath, in the Philistine country, and would have marched on up to Jerusalem if the king had not emulated the example of his ancestor, Asa (I Kings 15:18), and used the treasures of the Temple to purchase safety for himself and his people.

The assassination of Jehoash (vss. 20-21) is unexplained in Kings, but the Chronicler adds some information which may well have a good foundation of truth (II Chron. 24:15-22, 25-26). He states that after the death of Jehoiada, a conflict between the king and Jehoiada's son, Zechariah, ended with Zechariah's delivering a fiery speech against the king and his subsequent assassination on the king's orders. It is quite possible that such an incident may have led to the assassination of the king himself by partisans of the priesthood.

The history of Judah is continued in chapter 14.

The Weak Reign of Jehoahaz in Israel (13:1-9)

The catastrophic decline of Israel's power, which had begun so noticeably under Jehu (10:29-36), continued under the rule of his son, Jehoahaz, until the nation reached the nadir of impotence. If verse 3 is taken literally, as may well be correct, Israel during this period was little more than a vassal of Syria. The strength of her military forces was reduced to pitiful dimensions, as evidenced by the fact that she was left with only fifty horsemen and ten chariots. Verses 4 and 5 are difficult to understand in the general context; they look like an interpolation by a later editor who, for some reason, wanted to give a more favorable picture of the accomplishments of Jehoahaz. The account is so vague, however, that one can make little of it; the "savior" of whom the passage speaks has been variously supposed to be an Assyrian king who attacked Damascus and thereby created a diversion in Israel's favor (see the comment on vss. 22-25), or Jehoahaz' grandson, Jeroboam II, who at length succeeded in restoring the power and prestige of the nation. The purely mechanical way in which the Deuteronomic editors sometimes use their formulas is shown by the unintentional irony of the word "might" used of Jehoahaz in verse 8.

The Energetic Reign of Jehoash in Israel; Elisha's Death (13:10-25)

Under Jehoahaz' son, Jehoash (also called Joash, vs. 12), Israel began to recover some of the ground she had lost under the first two kings of Jehu's dynasty. This is not evident from the Deuteronomic summary found in verses 10-13 (and partly repeated in 14:15-16), but it is definitely stated in verse 25, which is taken from one of the older sources, probably the "Chronicles of the Kings of Israel" mentioned in verse 12. The major part of the space allotted to the reign of Jehoash is taken up with an account of the death of the prophet Elisha, who last appeared in the story in connection with Jehu's revolt, some forty years previously (9:1). It is reported that during Elisha's last illness he received a friendly visit from King Jehoash, who came to lament over him with the same words Elisha once had used of his master Elijah (2:12), "My father, my father! The chariots of Israel and its horsemen!"—meaning that Elisha was worth more to Israel than battalions of soldiers. Elisha made use of the opportunity to put his marvelous powers at the disposal of the nation for the last time. The symbolic act which follows is of a semimagical character and similar to acted parables elsewhere in the Old Testament (see, for example, Exod. 17:8-13; Joshua 8:18; I Kings 22:11;

Jer. 19:10-11). With Elisha's hand resting upon his, the king was commanded to shoot an arrow—identified by the prophet as "The LORD's arrow of victory"—eastward toward Transjordan, the Israelite territory still in Syrian hands. This was both a symbol and a pledge of victory over the Syrians. Then Elisha ordered the king to take the remaining arrows and strike them on the ground. He did so, but struck only three times. His failure to do it five or six times angered the prophet, who told him that his lack of vigor portended only a limited victory for Israel. It may be that the story correctly reflects a certain native deficiency in firmness and decision on the part of Jehoash, although these qualities are certainly not lacking in the account of his brief war with Judah found in the following chapter (14:8-14), which is, however, from a different source.

Even after Elisha's death his miraculous power clung to him. A popular story (the last of the Elijah-Elisha cycle) relates how a funeral was once interrupted by the appearance of a band of Moabite raiders; the mourners, instead of completing the ceremonies as planned, hurriedly placed the body in a nearby rock tomb which happened to be the burial place of Elisha. As soon as the corpse touched the prophet's body, life was restored, and the dead man rose to his feet (vss. 20-21).

The remaining verses (vss. 22-25) tell of Israel's recovery from the long series of humiliating reverses she had suffered at the hand of Syria. From sources outside the Bible we know that her renascence was due less to the greater ability of the new king than to the rising power of Assyria, one of whose rulers, Adad-nirari III (possibly the "savior" of 13:5), subjugated Damascus along with other adjoining regions in 805 B.C. shortly before the accession of Jehoash, and thus severely crippled Syria's military capabilities. Hazael died, and during the reign of his son, Ben-hadad, Jehoash recovered most of the territory Israel had previously lost. The way was now prepared for the spectacular power and prosperity which Israel would enjoy under Jehoash's son, Jeroboam II, the story of whose reign is related at the end of the next chapter (14:23-29).

The Vigorous Reign of Amaziah in Judah (14:1-22)

We now return briefly to the Southern Kingdom to see what happened after the assassination of Jehoash (Joash) of Judah.

Amaziah, the new king, seems to have been a worthy son of his father, and his reign is evaluated by the Deuteronomists in precisely the same way. The modern reader will probably place him even higher, for verses 5 and 6 indicate that he was a man of genuine spiritual sensitivity in whose reign a great ethical advance was made. The idea of the solidarity of the human social group had always been so strong in Israel that ordinarily, in the case of a serious crime such as sacrilege or the assassination of a king, the children of a criminal would be executed along with the criminal himself. (A good example is that of Achan in Joshua 7: 24-25. God himself is sometimes said to act on this principle; see Exodus 34:7 and Numbers 16:29-33.) This, however, Amaziah refused to do: "he did not put to death the children of the murderers" (vs. 6). This is said to have been in accordance with the law of Moses found in Deuteronomy (24:16), but historians are generally of the opinion that the law is actually later. If that is so, then Amaziah's generous act is one of the first manifestations of the growth in Israel of an ethical sense responsive to the realities of the human situation and to the just needs of individuals; the Deuteronomic law would be a later crystallization in statute form of this more enlightened conscience. While the religion of Israel remained essentially the same in basic character throughout the Old Testament period, it had within itself the seeds of this kind of ethical and spiritual growth; in this fact lay its immeasurable superiority to the cult of Baal-Melkart or any of the other religions of the ancient Near East.

The ambition and vigor of Amaziah are shown by his successful attack on Edom (vs. 7), which ever since the days of Jehoram (8:20-22) had been independent of Judah and blocked her access to the Red Sea. Amaziah was able to take her capital city of Sela (probably to be identified with a high fortified rock in the Petra area), thus breaking the power of Edom and making it possible to reopen the old trade route to the Gulf of Aqabah on which so much of Solomon's wealth had depended (I Kings 9:26-28).

The ambition of Amaziah took a less fortunate turn when he decided he was strong enough to defeat Israel also. Since the days of Ahab, Judah had been almost in a state of vassalage to Israel (see I Kings 22:2-4; II Kings 3:7; 8:18, 28), and the sense of inferiority no doubt rankled in the mind of a strong king like Amaziah, especially after he had shown his prowess in the war with the Edomites. So he unwisely issued a direct challenge to Jehoash of Israel, which Jehoash was not slow to answer. The Israelite king first gave an incisive warning to Amaziah by means of a fable in which he compared himself to a great cedar of Lebanon and the king of Judah to a little thistle in danger of being crushed by any passing beast. (For a somewhat similar fable, the only other in the Old Testament, see Judges 9:7-15.) But Amaziah was not to be deterred short of actual conflict, so a battle took place at Beth-shemesh, a few miles west of Jerusalem, in which the Judean army was so soundly trounced that Jehoash was able to enter Jerusalem, break down several hundred feet of the city wall, and rob the Temple of its treasures. He then returned triumphantly to Samaria with hostages.

For some reason which is not explained but which may have had its roots in the controversy that destroyed his father, a well-laid conspiracy was organized against Amaziah many years after the events described above and he was forced to flee, probably in the hope of finding a temporary refuge in Egypt (vs. 19). But at Lachish, some thirty-five miles southwest of Jerusalem, his enemies overtook and killed him. His son Azariah was then placed on the throne. The story of his reign is related in the following chapter (15:1-7), but a single important item, his rebuilding of the port of Elath at the head of the Gulf of Aqabah, is mentioned here (vs. 22).

The Long, Prosperous Reign of Jeroboam II in Israel (14:23-29)

The account of this reign provides another typical example of the way in which the Deuteronomists unintentionally color the historical perspective because of their preoccupation with matters of religion and morality. Although by all the standards of secular history Jeroboam was one of the most important kings of Israel, a ruler under whom for over forty years the Northern Kingdom enjoyed unprecedented prosperity and held dominion over an empire comparable in some respects to that of Solomon, the Second Book of Kings dismisses him in seven verses, four of which constitute the ordinary opening and closing formulas for the reigns of the kings of Israel.

The only concrete item recorded for Jeroboam's reign is that of his great success in extending the borders of his kingdom. His father, Jehoash, had recovered Transjordan from Syria, but Jeroboam managed to re-establish Israel's control over all the territory from "the entrance of Hamath" (the southern end of the valley between the Lebanon and Anti-Lebanon mountains) to "the Sea of the Arabah," the Dead Sea (the Arabah being the great rift which extends from the Dead Sea to the Gulf of Aqabah). Verse 28 says that his kingdom included Hamath, a city considerably north of Damascus, and Damascus itself. Neither of these statements is very probable, although Jeroboam may have been able to win again certain commercial privileges which Israel had once had in Damascus (I Kings 20:34). These accomplishments are said to have been in fulfillment of an oracle pronounced by the prophet Jonah, of Gath-hepher in Galilee. This prophet was evidently an extreme nationalist, one of those professional prophets of victory and prosperity against whom the later great prophets contended so vigorously; in the period after the Babylonian Exile an unknown author made him the chief character of the little Book of Jonah, in which his brand of narrow, nationalistic religion is caricatured in scathing, unforgettable terms.

One of the real mysteries of the Bible is why the Deuteronomists, whose interests were so exclusively religious, should have neglected to mention that Jeroboam's reign saw the beginning of the succession of the "literary" prophets—that is, of prophets whose oracles have been preserved for us in books. Both Amos and Hosea, the first two in this line and the only ones who worked in the Northern Kingdom, carried on their prophetic activity during this period (Amos 1:1; Hosea 1:1). Both of them, unlike the prophet Jonah, announced doom to Jeroboam and to the whole dynasty of Jehu. Amos came into direct conflict with the king (Amos 7:10-17; see also Hosea 1:4). From their books we get a lively impression of both the prosperity of Israel at this time (Amos 6:4-6; Hosea 10:1) and its basic moral corruption (Amos 2:6-8; Hosea 4:1-2). We are fortunate indeed in being able to supplement the Deuteronomists' historical record with these firsthand documents. Since the evidence they provide would have been excellent grist for the Deuteronomists' mill, we can only suppose that neither the names nor the collected oracles of these two prophets were known in Judah at the time the Books of Kings were written.

The Long, Prosperous Reign of Azariah (Uzziah) in Judah (15:1-7)

In 14:22 it is recorded that Azariah, the son of the murdered Amaziah, rebuilt the seaport of Elath and thereby restored the Red Sea trade. This fact is typical of his fifty-two-year reign, which was marked by the same kind of prosperity as that enjoyed by Israel under his contemporary, Jeroboam II. Further information is given by the Chronicler, who, at this point at any rate, must have had access to other good historical sources. He tells of successful campaigns against the Philistines and Arabs and of the tribute paid by the Ammonites, as well as of the king's building program in Jerusalem and elsewhere, and of his interest in agriculture and the development of the nation's military strength (II Chron. 26:6-15). A source of confusion for the ordinary reader is that this king, for reasons which can be only guessed at, is known by two different names, Azariah and Uzziah (compare, for example, 15:1 and 15:13). The Chronicler uses only the name Uzziah (II Chron. 26:1). We are told nothing further of the half-century during which Azariah-Uzziah reigned, beyond the fact that during his later years the king suffered from leprosy and the actual powers of government were placed in the hands of his son, Jotham. In characteristic fashion, the Chronicler adds a theological note to the story, explaining the disease as a punishment which God inflicted upon the king for his presumption in usurping the priestly privilege of offering incense in the Temple (II Chron. 26:16-21).

The history of Judah continues in 15:32 with the account of Jotham's accession to full kingship. It was in the year of the death of Azariah-Uzziah that Isaiah received his call to become a prophet of the Lord (Isa. 6:1). The Chronicler also reports that Isaiah was the author of a biography of the king (II Chron. 26:22).

The Brief Reign of Zechariah in Israel (15:8-12)

The great prosperity of Israel during the long reign of Jeroboam II was, as Amos and Hosea had so clearly seen, merely the rotten-ripeness of the fruit before it falls. The petition, "In all time of our prosperity, Good Lord, deliver us," is a prayer which greatly needs to be prayed, for prosperity subjects both men and nations to a far severer test than does adversity. Most men have reserves of natural courage which enable them to meet disaster, but only a few have the moral stamina to pass through a long period of good fortune unscathed by greed, pride, materialism, self-sufficiency, and indifference to the needs of others. Certainly both Israel and Judah failed this test, and it was the mission of Amos and Hosea in Israel, as of Isaiah and his successors in the Southern Kingdom, to announce the fact of their failure. Amos and Hosea saw quite clearly that the moral and religious foundations of Israel's life were so deeply undermined that her final doom could not be far in the future (Amos 3:13-15; 7:7-9; Hosea 5:8-14; 13:15-16; "Ephraim" is another common name for the Northern Kingdom). What remains of the history of Israel is the sad tale of her rapid fall into anarchy and her final dissolution as a nation.

Jeroboam II was succeeded by his son Zechariah, the last king of the dynasty of Jehu to sit upon the throne of Israel. His assassination after a reign of only six months is taken to be the fulfillment of an oracle spoken to Jehu nearly a hundred years before (vs. 12; compare 10:30); it fulfilled also the first part of Hosea's prophecy of doom made only a short time previously (Hosea 1:4).

The Very Brief Reign of Shallum in Israel (15:13-16)

The assassin and usurper, Shallum, lived only a month to enjoy his stolen throne, and he in turn was murdered by Menahem, a citizen of the former capital at Tirzah, who by calculated cruelty discouraged any resistance to his seizure of power (vs. 16). The sometimes mechanical character of the editing of this book is shown by the introduction of the usual formulas in connection with these brief reigns, where they can serve no purpose except to conceal the lack of real information (note vss. 9, 11, 15).

During this one year (747 B.C.) four kings were on the throne of Israel, and two of them met violent deaths.

The Reigns of Menahem and Pekahiah in Israel (15:17-26)

Of these latter kings of Israel only Menahem was able to pass the throne on to his son and thus make even a tentative gesture toward founding a dynasty. Only one event is reported of his ten-year reign—the payment of tribute to Assyria—but it was one of greatest consequence for the future history of both the kingdoms. All the rest of biblical history was to be enacted within the framework of one or another of the great world empires: first Assyria, then in succession, Babylonia, Persia, Greece, and Rome. It was under the shadow of the first three of these that the classical prophets received their message and converted the national religion of Israel into a religion with world-wide horizons and, at least potentially, a world-wide mission. Even for the common man, the God of Israel became the universal ruler of history and arbiter of the fate of all nations. This did not happen, of course, all at once, but the first step toward creating a situation favorable to that development was taken when Menahem agreed to pay tribute to the king of Assyria, thus recognizing him as Israel's overlord. (Jehu's payment of tribute had been only a temporary expedient.) Within a few years Assyria destroyed Israel and made Judah also a vassal kingdom. None of this at the time would have seemed propitious for the growth of high religion, and yet it is one of the unquestionable facts of history that, humanly speaking, the universal *religion* of the finest parts of the Old Testament was the product of the mental struggle of Israel's great spiritual teachers with the idea of a universal *empire* (see the comment on 19:25-28). The Assyrian king "Pul" in this passage is identical with the "Tiglath-pileser" (III) of verse 29; as ruler of a dual empire, he was known by the former name in Babylonia and by the latter in Assyria itself. The tax levied on the wealthy men was in the amount of thirty to thirty-five dollars, though allowance must be made for a tremendous difference in purchasing power, and there were evidently about 60,000 in Israel wealthy enough to pay—a vivid commentary on the prosperity of the times. The payment of this tribute is confirmed by Assyrian records.

Menahem's son, Pekahiah, occupied the throne for only two years before he was assassinated by Pekah, an officer in his army, who was obviously the leader of the faction favoring armed resistance to the demands of Assyria.

The Disastrous Reign of Pekah in Israel (15:27-31)

Historians universally regard the "twenty" years assigned to Pekah (vs. 27) as an ancient error; "two" would be more likely.

This king attempted to create an alliance of Syria, Israel, and Judah to withstand Assyria, but the refusal of Judah to have anything to do with so foolish a project led to the brief Syro-Ephraimite War which is mentioned in verse 37 and, with some note of its consequences, in the following chapter (16:5). The account of Pekah's reign tells only of Assyria's reaction, which was to strip from Israel all her lands in Transjordan and Galilee, reducing her to little more than a city-state consisting of Samaria and the territory immediately adjoining. Pekah was assassinated by a certain Hoshea who, backed by Assyrian arms, ascended the throne to become the last king of Israel. These events are also recorded in Assyrian annals. Hoshea's story is told in chapter 17.

The Reign of Jotham in Judah (15:32-38)

Meanwhile in Judah the leper king, Azariah-Uzziah, had been succeeded by his son, Jotham, who had already been regent for his invalid father for many years. Nothing is reported of his reign except the building of a new Temple gate (vs. 35) and the first moves which led to the Syro-Ephraimite War (vs. 37). The Chronicler adds, probably on the basis of good information, some details about building operations elsewhere in the kingdom and the successful subjugation of the Ammonites (II Chron. 27:4-5).

The Evil Reign of Ahaz in Judah (16:1-20)

Ahaz receives the unqualified condemnation of the editors of the Books of Kings because, probably for reasons which were more political than religious, he revived some of the discarded practices of ancient Semitic religion and also introduced for the first time new practices from Assyrian religion. Verse 3 states that he offered his own son as a sacrifice, just as the king of Moab had once done in a desperate emergency (3:27). The chief event of Ahaz' reign was the Syro-Ephraimite War. Judah was a small nation, and it seemed unlikely that it could withstand the assault of its two stronger neighbors, Syria and Israel, who were trying to force Ahaz into an alliance against the rising power of Assyria. According to the Chronicler, the opening phase of the war was a good deal more disastrous for Judah than one would suppose from Second Kings, and many captives were taken (II Chron. 28:5-15). The fear which the king and his peo-

ple felt is vividly portrayed in the book of the prophet Isaiah:
the heart of the king and his people "shook as the trees of the
forest shake before the wind" (Isa. 7:1-2). Isaiah's sound advice
was simply to put their trust in the God who had so often saved
them in the past (Isa. 7:4-9). But Ahaz was not convinced and
determined to follow what he would have considered a more
forthright and practical plan. First of all, he probably sacrificed
his son; but even superstition was not enough to quiet his mind,
so he then threw himself upon the mercy of the Assyrians and
begged them to come to his aid. This was the policy of depending upon foreign alliances to which the great prophets were so
violently opposed (Hosea 7:8-10; Isa. 30:1-5). Ahaz voluntarily
offered to become the vassal of the Assyrian king and sent him
the treasures of the Temple as tribute, with the result that the
Assyrians began a diversionary attack upon Damascus and thus
forced the allies to withdraw their armies from the siege of Jerusalem. Damascus soon fell, and the Syrian kingdom ceased to
exist except as a province of the Assyrian empire. (Isaiah 17:1-3
deals with this event.) Verse 6 is confusing, since in the Hebrew
it seems to be about the Syrians (see margin), but most students
are agreed that there is an error here in the Hebrew and that it
really has to do with the Edomites, who finally succeeded in re-
versing the victories won by Amaziah and Azariah (14:7; 14:22)
and so gained permanent control of the Red Sea trade (compare
II Chron. 28:17; notice that in the next verse the Chronicler also
tells of defeats by the Philistines).

Now saved from his neighbors, and with Damascus securely
in the hands of the Assyrians, Ahaz went to the former Syrian
capital to pay personal homage to his new master, Tiglath-pileser.
As a sign of the incorporation of his kingdom into the Assyrian
sphere of influence he ordered the introduction into the Temple
at Jerusalem of a new altar, undoubtedly of Assyrian pattern
and associated with the practices of Assyro-Babylonian religion.
This was not so much an expression of religious conviction as an
act of political necessity: it signified the loyalty of the king to the
Assyrian emperor. Of course the effect of such an innovation on
the religion of Judah would have been ultimately quite as damaging as the innovations of Jezebel in the Northern Kingdom, so
the southern prophets had to contend quite as vigorously against
influences from Assyrian religion as against the continuing sur-
vivals of the old Canaanite nature cult. The last part of verse 15

refers to the introduction of the Assyro-Babylonian practice of
trying to read the future by examining the entrails of sacrificial
animals. The cost of submission to Assyria is indicated by the necessity of destroying some of the bronze work in the Temple in
order to obtain further funds for the payment of tribute (vs. 17).
Verse 18 can no longer be understood.

The End of the Kingdom of Israel; Hoshea's Reign (17:1-23)

Now, for the last time, we take another look at developments
in the Northern Kingdom. It will be remembered that Hoshea
became king of Israel with the help and blessing of the Assyrians
(15:29-30). Here, however, we are introduced to a new factor in
the international situation, the growing ambition of Egypt, which
was the great rival of Assyria in the struggle for world dominion.
During the next century and a half, first Israel and then Judah
was torn with indecision. Should they live quietly by themselves
and trust in God, as the prophets taught, or should they ally themselves with one of the great world powers? If they chose the latter
course, should they accept the help of Egypt, or of Assyria? The
prophet Hosea pictures Israel as a foolish bird flitting back and
forth indecisively between the two great powers (Hosea 7:11).
The Egyptians managed to convince King Hoshea that by ally-
ing himself with them he could win Israel's freedom from Assyria,
so Hoshea unwisely rebelled against his overlord and refused to
pay tribute. The Assyrians under their new king, Shalmaneser V,
promptly invaded Israel and laid siege to Samaria. The strength
of Samaria's military situation is shown by the fact that the siege
lasted for three years; but the cause was hopeless, and finally under yet another new king, the usurper Sargon (as we learn from
Sargon's own account), the Assyrian army captured the city and
carried a large part of the population of Israel away into captivity. This was the end of the Northern Kingdom; henceforth
the region around the old capital would be known simply as the
Assyrian province of Samaria. The ten tribes which Jeroboam
I had formed into a kingdom would, throughout all subsequent
history, be called "the ten lost tribes" of Israel. Actually they
were never lost, in the sense in which the term is commonly used.
Many of the people remained in the land (Sargon speaks of having carried away only 27,590), and their descendants helped to

form the later community of the Samaritans: those who were transported to Assyria undoubtedly settled down and were eventually assimilated by the people among whom they lived. Modern speculations which attempt to identify the "lost tribes" with the British people (the "British-Israel" theory), the American Indians, or any other group are quite without foundation in historical fact.

In verses 7-23 the Deuteronomic editors introduce a long theological explanation of the catastrophic end of the kingdom of Israel. For them it was the just punishment of Israel's long record of disloyalty to God. The Deuteronomists composed the Books of Kings in order to show how loyalty to God is the one great principle which should govern the life of his people; the fall of Israel is for them the first great and overwhelming proof that this is so.

The Founding of the Samaritan Community (17:24-41)

Verses 24-28 tell how the Assyrians settled foreigners from other parts of their empire in the land vacated by the Israelites (Sargon's account also confirms this part of the biblical record). The passage is of great incidental interest in showing how people of the ancient world believed that gods were attached to particular localities. The new inhabitants interpreted some disasters which befell them during the early period of their settlement as resulting from their ignorance of the manner in which "the god of the land" should be worshiped. So they asked for instruction and became, at least in an external and superficial sense, servants of the God of Israel. The Samaritans of the New Testament are the descendants of the old population of the kingdom of Israel mixed to some extent with these foreigners who came and settled amongst them. Verses 29-41 are an expansion of this passage by the Deuteronomic editors, who explain that the worship of this new, mixed people (who can now be called simply "Samaritans") was really a kind of syncretism in which the true worship of the Lord was adulterated by the worship of all kinds of foreign gods whom the settlers brought with them.

THE REMAINING HISTORY OF THE KINGDOM OF JUDAH

II Kings 18:1—25:21

The Good Reign of Hezekiah (18:1—20:21)

Hezekiah's Reform (18:1-12)

As has been previously noted, the history of Judah from this point on is determined by a struggle among three parties, each trying to influence national policy. First, there was the party which favored strict loyalty to the God of Israel and believed that the safety of the kingdom depended upon trust in him rather than in foreign alliances of any kind. We may call this the *prophetic* party because its principles were those of the great prophets Isaiah, Micah, and Jeremiah. Their motto was, in effect, the familiar words of Isaiah,

"In returning and rest you shall be saved;
in quietness and in trust shall be your strength" (Isa. 30:15).

Second, there was the *pro-Assyrian* (later pro-Babylonian) party which favored an alliance with the great empire of the East. Finally, there was the *pro-Egyptian* party which believed that greater benefits would be derived from dependence on Egypt, Judah's neighbor to the south. In Ahaz' reign the pro-Assyrian party had come to power; but under his son, Hezekiah, a reaction took place in favor of the prophetic party, perhaps due primarily to the powerful influence of the prophet Isaiah, whose ministry spanned the whole twenty-nine years of Hezekiah's reign and who was held in great respect by the king. Hezekiah has the unqualified approval of the Deuteronomist editors because he inaugurated a movement to purify the worship of the Lord from the remaining traces of the old Canaanite fertility religion. Whether his reform was quite as extensive as is here represented is still a matter of dispute, but there can be no doubt that he eliminated Canaanite cultic objects from the Temple at Jerusalem. It is especially interesting to notice that he destroyed the ancient bronze serpent called Nehushtan, which tradition associated with Moses (Num. 21: 8-9) but which, for the popular mind, was an object of superstitious veneration. Like Ahaz' introduction of Assyrian practices in the Temple, Hezekiah's reform necessarily had political significance also, so we are not surprised to learn that he "rebelled against the king of Assyria" (vs. 7). His war against the Philistines was a phase of this revolt. Most of the remainder of Hezekiah's story is taken up with an account of the Assyrian attempt to force him into submission. The chronological relationship of these events is not entirely clear. As the story is told in Kings one would suppose that the reform occurred near the beginning of Hezekiah's reign, whereas we know that the siege of Sennacherib did not take place until 701 B.C., near the end. We should probably think of the reform as actually taking place not long before that date. From Isaiah 20 we learn also of another occasion (in 711 B.C.) when a united revolt of Assyria's western vassal states was projected; Isaiah was strongly opposed to having Hezekiah join it. These scattered facts remind us of how fragmentary our knowledge of ancient Hebrew history really is. Verses 9-12 are a summary of the last days of the kingdom of Israel, which overlapped the beginning of Hezekiah's reign.

Sennacherib's Invasion (18:13—19:37)

The long, detailed account of the Assyrian invasion is mostly taken from a popular, prophetic document not very different in character from the one which contained the Elijah-Elisha stories; the prophet Isaiah is the hero and, for that reason, this whole section (minus 18:14-16) was later added to his collected oracles (Isa. 36-37; see also II Kings 20 and Isa. 38-39). Sennacherib, who had succeeded Sargon as king of Assyria, took stern measures to suppress the revolt in his western territories. His capture of the city of Lachish, southwest of Jerusalem, is vividly pictured in a famous relief found on the walls of his palace at Nineveh. Archaeology has also brought to light Sennacherib's own account of his campaign against Judah, in which he says he shut up Hezekiah in Jerusalem "like a bird in a cage." The statements in 18:14-16 (omitted in Isaiah 36-37), which tell of Hezekiah's submission and payment of tribute, closely agree with Sennacherib's own story. The rest of the narrative, told in a more racy, popular style, represents Hezekiah as resisting Sennacherib's demands and being finally delivered by a miracle (19:35). It is possible, as some historians think, that the editors have telescoped accounts of two different campaigns.

The account in 18:17—19:7 gives in fascinating detail the story of an embassy under the direction of three Assyrian officers

(whose official titles are given) sent from Lachish to Jerusalem
to demand the surrender of the city. They met three officials of
Hezekiah (whose titles are also given) at the same place outside
the walls where Isaiah had once conferred with King Ahaz (Isa.
7:3). They warned the king that he could expect no help from
Egypt (vss. 19-21); that the Lord, whose sanctuaries had been
sacrilegiously destroyed by Hezekiah's reform, could hardly be
expected to protect him (vs. 22); and that his forces were ridicu-
lously weak as compared with those of Assyria (vss. 23-24). Sennacherib has come, they say, in obedience to the Lord, who is
angry with his people (vs. 25; for this idea, compare 17:18 and
Isa. 10:5). The speech was a clever one, a fine example of ancient psychological warfare. It was so clever, in fact, that Hezekiah's representatives asked the Assyrians please not to speak
any more in Hebrew, which the common people nearby could
understand, but rather to speak the unfamiliar Aramaic, which
at this time was becoming the diplomatic language of the ancient
Near East (vs. 26). The chief of the Assyrian delegation, de-
lighted with his success, refused and turned to address the populace directly (vs. 27). He warns them of Hezekiah's impotence
(vss. 28-30), promises them generous treatment at Sennacherib's
hands (vss. 31-32), and asserts that their God is no more able
to deliver them than the gods of other nations whom the Assyrians have conquered (vss. 33-35). Although the people ex-
hibited no immediate reaction, Hezekiah's messengers returned
to him shaken and desperate (vss. 36-37). Hezekiah was equally
shaken and sent a deputation clothed in sackcloth to Isaiah to
inform him of the situation and beg for his prayers (19:1-5).
Isaiah's reply was an oracle of encouragement: the Lord would
soon cause the Assyrian king to receive bad news which would
impel him to return home, and there he would die (19:6-7).

The relationship between 18:17—19:7 and 19:8-36 is another
of the problems presented by these chapters. Some interpreters
think that we have here duplicate, but variant, accounts of the
same events. The editors of Kings, however, undoubtedly understood the second account to be the sequel of the first. According
to this view, the first Assyrian embassy returned to Sennacherib
without having accomplished its purpose. Then, a second one was
sent at a later time when the Assyrian king heard that Tirhakah,
the Ethiopian king of Egypt, was advancing to fight against him
(19:8-9). This deputation brought a letter for Hezekiah which

warned him not to put any foolish trust in the Lord, for none of the gods of other nations had ever been able to save their people from being conquered by the Assyrians (vss. 10-13). On this occasion Hezekiah took the letter into the Temple to show to God, and himself offered a prayer asking the Lord to save his people and thus demonstrate to all nations that the gods of other races were no gods at all, that he alone was "the living God" (vss. 14-19). This time, of his own volition, Isaiah sent a long encouraging oracle to the king (vss. 20-34). It begins with a dramatic picture of Jerusalem ("the virgin daughter of Zion") hurling her scornful defiance at the Assyrian king (vs. 21), who is warned that the God of whom his letter speaks so contemptuously is "the Holy One of Israel," this being one of Isaiah's favorite names for the Lord (see, for example, Isa. 5:19, 24; 17:7). The idea of God's "holiness" is intended to convey some sense of his unapproachable majesty and incomparable power (see Isa. 6:3-5). Then the prophet mockingly echoes the language of Assyrian inscriptions in which kings boasted of the victories they had won. Sennacherib is represented as using this kind of language to threaten his western adversaries and announce his plan of advancing even into Egypt (vss. 23-24). The Revised Standard Version, translating the Hebrew words literally, makes the verbs of verses 23 and 24 past tense. The Hebrew language, however, often uses the past tense of the verb, especially in the language of prophecy, to represent future events which are certain to occur. Since Assyria had not conquered Egypt at this time, the *sense* of the verbs must be future. The prophet then goes on (vss. 25-28) to declare that any victory which the Assyrians had won in the past had been due solely to God's power and permission. Here is an excellent illustration of the way in which Israel's great spiritual leaders were brought to the knowledge of the Lord's universal power by being confronted with the fact of a universal empire (see comment on 15:19). The argument in their minds would have run something like this: Victory belongs to the nation which has the most powerful gods (everyone in the ancient Near East would have agreed with this principle). Therefore, if the people of the Lord are defeated by Assyrian armies, this ought to mean that the gods of the Assyrians are more powerful than he. But this is an impossible conclusion, because the prophets of the Lord have an unshakable faith, based upon their experience and the ancient experiences of their people, that the Lord's power is really unconquerable. The only alternative—and this was a daring and original hypothesis—was that an all-powerful Lord was using the Assyrians for his own great purposes: that he himself had brought them onto the soil of Judah to punish his people for their sins. This would mean that the Lord was really the *only* God—the God of the Assyrians as well as of the Jews. The Assyrians were in the process of carving out a universal empire, but this was possible only because the Holy One of Israel was the universal God. The Assyrians, of course, did not realize this; they attributed their victories to the power of their own weapons and despised the ineffectual little god of a little land. Their turn, however, soon would come. The Lord would not long tolerate their pride and cruelty; he would put a hook in their nose (as though they were cattle) and lead them back where they came from. The Book of Isaiah (10:5-19) contains the classic exposition of this theme.

Thus far the oracle is in poetry, as are most of the oracles of the prophets, but verses 29-34 are in prose. This section contains a more explicit account of what is to happen in the immediate future. There will be a gradual return to prosperity over a two-year period, with everything back to normal by the third year (vs. 29). One of the worst effects of an invasion such as that of Sennacherib was, of course, the disruption of agricultural operations and the famine which would necessarily ensue. In verses 30-31 we meet with one of the favorite ideas of the Book of Isaiah and of the entire Bible: the idea that even though the greater part of the nation may be destroyed, God will always preserve a saved and saving "remnant" (see Isa. 1:9; 10:20-21; 11:11, 16; Rom. 11:4-5; see also the comment on I Kings 19:18). The importance of this concept in the mind of Isaiah is shown by the fact that one of his children was named Shear-jashub, meaning in Hebrew "a remnant shall return" (Isa. 7:3). The prose passage closes with a renewed affirmation of God's purpose to deliver Jerusalem (vss. 32-34).

The narrative then relates briefly the fulfillment of the promise. A mysterious affliction befell the Assyrian army during the night and killed 185,000 of them. Sennacherib gave up the siege and returned to his capital at Nineveh, where he was assassinated. The biblical account is very much condensed, for we know from Assyrian records that the king's murder did not take place until nearly twenty years later. The Assyrian documents contain no reference to any disaster which befell the army at Jerusalem, though the Greek historian Herodotus tells of a mysterious defeat of Sennacherib's forces at Pelusium on the borders of Egypt which may have been caused by an outbreak of the plague. Possibly the two stories have somehow become combined. Many interpreters think that the real reason for Sennacherib's sudden return to Assyria was that he received news of increasing disaffection at home; this would accord better with the prophecy in 19:7. In any event, the salient fact for the people of Judah was that Sennacherib's siege of Jerusalem had failed—contrary to all the logic of the military situation. They could only consider this as renewed evidence of God's loving care for his people. It may be that Isaiah 17:12-14 is a poetic account of this deliverance, just as Isaiah 22:1-14 may reflect Isaiah's later disappointment with the spiritual results of the nation's experience at this time. The siege, instead of bringing the people to a mood of repentance, had caused them only to say, "Let us eat and drink, for tomorrow we die" (Isa. 22:13); and even their deliverance had not brought them any closer to God.

Hezekiah's Sickness (20:1-11)

Chapter 20 is introduced with the vague phrase "in those days." This tells us little. It seems probable, however, that the events now to be described took place sometime *before* Sennacherib's invasion in 701 B.C. (18:13—19:37). The embassy from Merodach-baladan, described in verses 12-19, is said to have been connected with Hezekiah's sickness (vs. 12), but, as we shall see, it must also have been related to the king's decision to rebel against his Assyrian overlord, and therefore would have to be dated sometime before the rebellion took place (18:7). Some interpreters would put the events of this chapter in 702 B.C.; others as early as 711 B.C.

When Hezekiah was taken ill, the prophet Isaiah, at God's instance, warned him that it was a sickness unto death, but the king's prayer for healing was so sincere that God determined to add fifteen years to his life. Isaiah, who had gone from the sickroom only as far as the courtyard of the palace when he received the second message from the Lord, came back to bring Hezekiah the good news. The story is an excellent illustration of the conviction of the men of the Bible that "the prayer of a righteous man has great power in its effects" (James 5:16). Isaiah, in accordance with ancient medical practice, administered a poultice, and the king soon recovered. Hezekiah asked for some evidence that the healing would be permanent, so the Lord gave him a sign, causing the shadow on the sun "dial" to go back ten degrees or "steps." This is the only reference in the Bible to a chronometer of any kind; in actuality the "dial" was probably an exterior stairway so arranged that the time of day could be determined by observing the sun's shadow on the steps.

The Embassy from Merodach-baladan (20:12-19)

The deputation sent from Merodach-baladan is here connected ostensibly with Hezekiah's recovery from illness. This may indeed have provided a suitable excuse for the visit, but the real reason was to try to induce the king to join a general revolt against Assyria. Merodach-baladan is well known from Assyrian sources as a rebel who successfully seized the city of Babylon and ruled there for a number of years in defiance of the Assyrians. He remained a thorn in their side for a long time, stirring up trouble in other vassal states. That this was the real purpose of the messengers in coming to Hezekiah is proved by their interest in the king's financial and military resources (vs. 13), and by Isaiah's unfriendly attitude toward them (vss. 14-18). Isaiah, like all the prophets, was consistently opposed to entangling foreign alliances.

Hezekiah's Improvements in the Water Supply (20:20-21)

Verses 20 and 21 are the Deuteronomic editors' customary concluding formula, adapted to the reign of Hezekiah, but the passage contains also the interesting information that Hezekiah constructed a conduit to bring water directly into Jerusalem. The "conduit" was a tunnel running through solid rock from Gihon (the modern "Virgin's Spring") outside the city wall to the Pool of Siloam, which was then located inside the wall. This was an important defensive measure which made the city better able to withstand a siege. The tunnel, over 1,700 feet long, is still to be seen in Jerusalem. In 1880 a now-famous inscription was found inside the tunnel which describes how it was built simultaneously from both ends, the diggers meeting in the middle.

The Chronicler tells of the tunnel in greater detail (II Chron.

32:30). Otherwise he has little additional information to contribute to our knowledge of Hezekiah's reign. He expands the brief account of the reform enormously with many embellishments (II Chron. 29-31), but he drastically abbreviates the story of Hezekiah's relations with Assyria told in II Kings 18:13— 20:19, omitting, for example, any mention of Merodach-baladan.

The Reactionary Reign of Manasseh (21:1-18)

Manasseh's reign of fifty-five years was the longest in the history of the Southern Kingdom, but the Deuteronomists have little to tell about any actual events because of their abhorrence of Manasseh's policies. The length of his reign was a problem for them because it seemed to refute the principle that disloyalty to God brings certain punishment in the form of disaster and early death. As we all know, the problem of the prosperity of the wicked and the suffering of the innocent is one of the greatest problems of life and far more complicated than the Deuteronomists indicated. Other books of the Bible, such as Habakkuk (see Hab. 1:13), Job (see Job 21:7-26), Ecclesiastes (see Eccles. 9:11-12), and Psalms (see Ps. 73), reveal the great struggle that went on in the souls of some of Israel's deepest thinkers over this very issue and their obvious dissatisfaction with the too literal way in which the Deuteronomists interpreted the principle of retribution. A more profound approach to the problem is to be found in the "suffering servant" passage in Isaiah (Isa. 52:13— 53:12), and in the New Testament understanding of the Cross. We must not, however, unfairly blame the Deuteronomists even though they conceived of the law of justice as operating in too simple a way and were somewhat baffled by life's apparent contradictions. It was their great merit that they had a secure grasp on the basic truth that God is just, and that wickedness is in some way inevitably punished while righteousness has its sure reward. Their trouble did not arise from too firm an adherence to this principle, but from the mechanical way in which they attempted to apply it to actual, and often very complex, human situations. In the present instance, the fall of the kingdom of Judah, which occurred about half a century after Manasseh's death, is interpreted as due to the sins which he had committed (see vss. 10-15 and 23:26). The Chronicler, on the other hand, represents Manasseh as having been brought to repent of his sins

during a period when he was held prisoner by the Assyrians
(II Chron. 33:10-13); because of this, the Chronicler says, God
forgave him and restored to him his throne. The whole problem
of undeserved punishments and rewards is not quite so difficult
for us as it was for the ancient Hebrews because of our belief
in a *future* life, a belief to which they had not yet attained in the
days when the Deuteronomists and the Chronicler wrote.

Manasseh's reign was marked by a violent reaction against the
policies of his father, Hezekiah. The pro-Assyrian party came to
power, and the prophetic party was driven underground. Many
believe that it was during this period, when the prophetic movement had to be carried on in secret, that the Book of Deuteronomy (or at least the legal code which is the heart of it) was
compiled to provide a basis for the great reform which at last
came into effect under King Josiah. (Notice how Deuteronomy
4:19; 17:3; and 18:10-11 point unmistakably to conditions in
Manasseh's time, as seen from a comparison with II Kings
21:5-6.) The story of Manasseh's reign, which is written entirely
in the characteristic language of the Deuteronomists, tells of
nothing but the king's activities in furthering the syncretistic kind
of religion which had been favored by Ahab of Israel and, more
recently, by Ahaz in Judah (see ch. 16). Manasseh restored the
practices of the old Canaanite fertility religion with its worship
of male and female gods and goddesses, introduced the cult of
the Assyrian astral gods ("the host of heaven"), and revived the
practice of child sacrifice. The adherents of the prophetic party
were mercilessly persecuted (vs. 16). According to an old
Jewish legend, which is probably referred to in Hebrews 11:37,
the prophet Isaiah was executed at this time by being "sawn in
two." Besides the story of Manasseh's imprisonment and subsequent repentance and reformation, the Chronicler has nothing
to add to this story except a note about some building operations
in Jerusalem and the stationing of military officials in "all the
fortified cities in Judah" (II Chron. 33:14). Manasseh died in
peace and was buried in his own garden (II Kings 21:18).

The Brief Reign of Amon (21:19-26)

Manasseh's son and successor made no change in the policies
of his father. After ruling only two years he was struck down by
a palace conspiracy, which failed to achieve its positive purpose

(whatever that may have been) because "the people of the land" revolted against the regicides and secured the throne for Amon's son, Josiah.

The Reforming Reign of Josiah (22:1—23:30)

With the accession of Josiah, the Deuteronomists arrive at the climax of their story. It was in his reign that the "Deuteronomic" reformation took place, so, understandably enough, they can hardly find words adequate to praise him; for them he was the paragon of kings (see vs. 2 and 23:25). Only Hezekiah was in any way comparable to him (18:3).

As is true of all the later reigns in Israel and Judah, internal events are not entirely comprehensible without some knowledge of the background of international history, since the fate of the small nations of the Levant was closely tied up with the rise and fall of great world empires. The preceding century (the eighth) had seen the rise of Assyria to a position of dominance in which she controlled all the Near East except Egypt. Later, during the early seventh century, when Manasseh was on the throne of Judah, Egypt itself had been conquered and added to the Assyrian realm; but soon after the middle of that century Assyria's power was definitely on the wane. Egypt was lost, and Assyrian control over the small states of the west became increasingly tenuous. It was in this period that Josiah came to the throne; his religious reformation was part of a great nationalistic rebirth which began to take shape as the fortunes of Assyria declined. Similar religious revivals seem to have occurred in both Egypt and Babylon at approximately the same time and for the same reason. With the death of Ashurbanipal, the last great Assyrian emperor, the Assyrian state began to disintegrate rapidly; it finally collapsed with the capture and destruction of Nineveh, the capital city, by the Babylonians, Medes, and Scythians in 612 B.C.—an event celebrated with great gusto by the Book of Nahum. Egypt and Babylonia then entered into competition for the privilege of succeeding to Assyria's role, and Josiah met his tragic death through an unfortunate involvement in the conflict between the two rival powers. Of these great movements and the tremendous issues which were being decided the Bible gives us no hint; its narrative nevertheless becomes more intelligible when the events of II Kings 22-23 are thus seen in full historical

120   SECOND KINGS 22:1-20

perspective as the reflection in Judah of a drama being played upon the international stage.

Josiah's Renovation of the Temple (22:1-7)

As had happened in the reign of Jehoash before him (12:4-16), Josiah's national revival found its first effective expression in a movement to restore and rehabilitate the Temple, which had been so long neglected by its royal guardian and polluted by the intrusion of imported gods and alien forms of worship. In the Chronicler's version the renovation of the Temple came as the climax of an effort at reform which had already been going on for ten years (II Chron. 34:3-8), but the narrative in Kings, which makes the great reformation an outgrowth of this first, tentative movement toward national and religious self-assertion, seems more likely to be correct.

The Discovery of the Book (22:8-20)

During the process of repairing the Temple a book was discovered which was destined to convert Josiah's rather superficial attempt at national renewal into a basic reformation which would affect every aspect of Israel's life and change the character of her religion for all time to come. Just what the book was, where it came from, and how it got there are among the most fundamental questions discussed by students of the Old Testament. As to what it was, there can hardly be any doubt that it was some form of the Book of Deuteronomy; the numerous points of agreement in both words and matter between the laws of Deuteronomy and the steps of the reform, especially with respect to the destruction of the "high places" (the local shrines) and the consequent limitation of sacrificial worship to the Temple in Jerusalem, cannot be readily explained on any other assumption. Where the book came from and how it got in the Temple are more difficult questions, but the most common view is that it was a compendium of ancient laws, traditionally ascribed to Moses, but collected, revised, and edited in a new spirit by members of the prophetic party during the reign of Manasseh, and then deposited in the Temple library with the hope that sometime it would be discovered and used as a program of national reform.

Nothing is told us as to precisely how it was found. It is said only that Hilkiah, the priest in charge of the Temple, announced its discovery to Shaphan the scribe, who then read it before the king. Josiah's reaction was one of terror and foreboding, occasioned no doubt by such words as those of Deuteronomy 28:15-68. He tore his clothes and ordered that the Lord should be consulted by the agency of one of his prophets (this is the meaning of "Go, inquire of the LORD," vs. 13), so that the king might learn what God's intentions were and what course of action he should take. In view of the fact that the prophet Zephaniah was active during the time of Josiah (Zeph. 1:1), and that Jeremiah, one of the greatest of the prophets, was called to an active ministry five years before this date (see Jer. 1:1-2), it seems strange that, instead of consulting either of these, the king's representatives went to the otherwise unknown prophetess Huldah to make their inquiry. The fact that they did so is a useful reminder of the truth that posterity often has a more accurate idea of a man's importance than do his contemporaries. Zephaniah and Jeremiah evidently did not seem important figures in the early years of Josiah's reign. The "Second Quarter" (vs. 14) probably refers to the northern extension of the city. Huldah's verdict was that the doom of the nation was at hand because of its long record of disloyalty to God and the principles set forth in the book. Although her oracle has probably been to some extent revised by the editors so as to conform more closely to the known course of events, this cannot be true of the promise in verse 20, which is contradicted by 23:29 and must therefore contain the actual words of the prophetess. The preservation of an unfulfilled prophecy in the text of the Deuteronomists' work is further testimony to their remarkable integrity as historians.

The Great Reformation (23:1-25)

The editors of the Books of Kings are called "the Deuteronomists" because the whole of their history—which includes all the books from Deuteronomy to Second Kings—was written in the light of the great revolution which Josiah effected on the basis of principles explicitly set forth in the Book of Deuteronomy. The judgments which they pass on the kings of Israel and Judah are based in each case upon the measure to which the individual king conformed or failed to conform to principles which, in their opinion, were not new but had been part of the fundamental charter of the nation from its very beginning. In broadest terms the Deuteronomic principle may be stated as "absolute loyalty to

the God of Israel." Put in slightly more specific language, it is
well summarized in the formula "one nation, one God, one
sanctuary." Israel was a *unique* nation because the Lord had
chosen it for his own out of all the nations of the earth (Deut.
7:6); he *alone*, therefore, must receive the worship of the people
of Israel to the exclusion of all other gods (Deut. 5:6-10; 6:4);
and, in order to preserve the oneness of Israel and the oneness
of her God, worship in the full sense (the observance of festivals
and offering of incense and sacrifice) must be permitted only in
the *one* sanctuary, the Temple at Jerusalem (Deut. 12:1-7).
Furthermore, the relationship of the one God to the one nation
through the one sanctuary was stabilized for all generations in
the form of a solemn "covenant" formally agreed upon between
the Lord and his people (Deut. 5:2-3). The Deuteronomists were
right, of course, in believing that something of this kind had
been the basis of Israel's existence from the start, although it had
never been so clearly and explicitly formulated before.

Chapter 23 begins by telling how Josiah put into effect the
program set forth in "the book." There was first of all a great
ceremony in Jerusalem at which the book was publicly read and
both king and people declared their adherence to the Covenant
which it proclaimed (vss. 1-3). Then the king inaugurated measures to put into force the laws of Deuteronomy which forbade
the worship of other gods, and the worship of the one God at
more than one sanctuary. The Temple was purified of all the
objects connected with the worship of the old Canaanite fertility
gods (Baal and Asherah) and the Assyro-Babylonian star gods
("the host of the heavens") (vss. 4-6, 8b, 11, 12, 14; compare
Deut. 17:2-5); the sacred prostitutes were driven out (vs. 7;
compare Deut. 23:17-18); the place of child sacrifice in the
Valley of Hinnom (Gehenna) to the west and south of Jerusalem
was defiled (vs. 10; compare Deut. 18:10); and the shrines
of foreign gods which stood on the Mount of Olives (here, by a
slight change in the Hebrew word, called "the mount of corruption") were destroyed (vs. 13). After the Temple and the
neighborhood of Jerusalem were freed from the worship of
foreign gods and from cultic practices foreign to the true nature
of Israel's God, Josiah turned his attention to the country districts and to the elimination of all sanctuaries except that in
Jerusalem itself. The country shrines ("the high places") were
so closely associated with the old Canaanite gods of fertility

and their immoral rites that it seemed impossible ever to purify them; the code of Deuteronomy solved the problem by the drastic measure of ordering them all to be destroyed and prohibiting formal worship—in particular the offering of sacrifice—anywhere except in the Temple at Jerusalem, where it would be under the watchful eye of priests completely loyal to the God of Israel and the traditional ways of honoring him (Deut. 12:2-7). So Josiah's next step was to destroy all the secondary shrines throughout the land (vss. 5, 15-20) and to make provision for incorporating the country priests into the Jerusalem priesthood (vs. 8a; compare Deut. 18:6-8). Since there were so many of these priests, he was not altogether successful in this latter effort (vs. 9); it is possible that these country priests were the ancestors of "the Levites" (the class just below the priesthood) in later Judaism. Verses 15-19 tell of the course of the reformation in Samaria, the territory of the old northern kingdom of Israel, which Josiah reincorporated into the kingdom of Judah following the collapse of Assyrian authority in the north. Bethel was, of course, one of the two principal shrines of the Northern Kingdom (I Kings 12:29). The incident in verses 16-18 refers to the story told in I Kings 13. If verse 20 is to be taken literally, the treatment of the northern priests was more drastic than that accorded to their counterparts in Judah.

The climax of the reformation was the celebration of a great Passover in accordance with the rules of "this book of the covenant" (vss. 21-23; compare Deut. 16:1-8). In the older laws (Exod. 12:21-27) it was ordered that the Passover should be celebrated at home, but Deuteronomy, in harmony with its centralizing tendencies, ordered that it should be observed only in Jerusalem (Deut. 16:5-6). Verse 24 notes that along with his other reforms Josiah also abolished witchcraft and other forms of superstition such as the use of little household images called teraphim (compare Deut. 18:10-11).

It is commonly believed that verse 25 (with the possible exception of the last clause) marks the end of the first edition of the Books of Kings, an edition published not long after the reform and in the full flush of its initial success.

The Tragic End of Josiah's Reign (23:26-30)

The material in II Kings 23:26—25:21 seems to have been added to the original Books of Kings in the days of the Babylonian Exile, when it had long been obvious that, from a political point of view, Josiah's reign had not marked the beginning of a golden age, as the original Deuteronomists had supposed, but rather, at least at the end, the first step toward the final catastrophe. So incredible was the disaster, and so hard to understand on the basis of Deuteronomic principles, that the historians could explain it only as a consequence of Manasseh's wickedness, which had been so great that even Josiah's valiant measures were unable to cancel Israel's guilt in the eyes of God (vs. 26 and 24:3-4). This line of reasoning, which involves punishing children for the sins of their fathers, may not commend itself to the Christian reader, nor did it to other thinkers in Israel (see Ezek. 18:1-4, 19-20, remembering that Ezekiel lived at the same time as the later Deuteronomists). But we can nevertheless sympathize deeply with the Deuteronomic thinkers in their effort to find some kind of rational and moral explanation of these terrible events. Even though Christians have the advantage of knowing certain great truths which were concealed from the Deuteronomists, the problem of "justifying the ways of God to man" is still, in many instances, a very difficult one. The New Testament itself suggests that the answer is not always simple (see John 9:1-3).

Josiah's reign, most of which had been so promising, came to a calamitous end. This is one of the cases in which the Chronicler's account (II Chron. 35:20-23) is fuller, probably accurate, and certainly more intelligible than the brief sentence in II Kings 23:29. During the years following the collapse of Assyria, Egypt was in competition with Babylon for control of world empire. Pharaoh Neco was leading his army to the north, there to give what support he could to the feeble remnant of the Assyrian kingdom against the rising Babylonians. Josiah, naturally opposed to any attempt at world dominion, apparently tried to stop him from getting through the pass at Megiddo, which was in the old territory of northern Israel and was now claimed for Judah. But the effort was futile and ill-advised, and Josiah himself died on the field of battle. "The people of the land" then chose one of his sons, Jehoahaz, to succeed him.

The Short Reign of Jehoahaz (23:31-35)

The reign of Jehoahaz is virtually a fiction, since the Egyptians were now in control of the situation and immediately deposed the popular choice in favor of his brother, Eliakim (whose name they changed to Jehoiakim), a man evidently more amenable to Egyptian control. Jehoahaz was taken to Egypt as a prisoner and died there. We have no record of the lament which Jeremiah is said to have composed for Josiah (II Chron. 35:25), but we still can read his lament for Jehoahaz in Jeremiah 22:10-12 (Jeremiah calls him "Shallum," the name he probably bore before his brief occupancy of the throne). The Egyptians imposed a heavy tribute on the kingdom (vs. 35).

The Evil Reign of Jehoiakim (23:36—24:7)

The evil character of Jehoiakim is fully confirmed by the prophet Jeremiah, who accused him of oppression and a selfish love of luxury—facts which were all the more shocking because of the contrast with the just and devout character of his father Josiah's rule (Jer. 22:13-19). Part of the Book of Jeremiah is devoted to the prophet's activity during the reign of Jehoiakim (Jer. 25; 26; 35; 45; 46:2-12); it also tells of the uncompromising antipathy between Jeremiah and the king (Jer. 36). Jeremiah was certainly an important public figure at this time, and it is strange that the editors of Kings, who must have been sympathetic to his position, make no mention of him (contrast II Chron. 35:25).

Although Jehoiakim reigned for eleven years, the Deuteronomists speak of him only in general terms except for a note about some border raids (24:2) and the brief statement that he rebelled against Babylon (vs. 1). In order to understand this latter statement, it is necessary to pursue a little further the course of international history. The Egyptians, after their defeat of Josiah, continued north and eventually (in 605 B.C.) came into direct conflict with the Babylonian forces under Nebuchadrezzar (as the name is properly spelled) at Carchemish, in northern Syria, where they were decisively defeated (24:7; II Chron. 35:20; Jer. 46:2-12). Inevitably Judah soon came under Babylonian control (vs. 1a). Some years later Jehoiakim seems to have felt strong enough, probably encouraged by the Egyptians, to rebel against his new overlords (vs. 1b). A Babylonian army was sent to bring him into submission, but before the siege of Jerusalem could effect its purpose Jehoiakim escaped the consequences of his folly by dying and was succeeded by his son Jehoiachin.

Jehoiachin's Reign and Captivity (24:8-17)

Jehoiakim's unfortunate son came to the throne at the age of eighteen (II Chron. 36:9 erroneously says "eight") and ruled only long enough to see the city captured by the imperial armies and himself taken off into captivity in Babylonia along with a large part of the nobility and the most useful members of the population (598 B.C.). The prophet Ezekiel was one of these exiles and carried on his entire prophetic ministry in Babylon. Verses 13-14 seem to be out of place here, being more appropriate as a description of the final punishment of the city ten years later. For Jeremiah's verdict on Jehoiachin (whom he calls "Coniah" or "Jeconiah," variant forms of the same name) see Jeremiah 22:24-30. The Babylonians asserted their authority by placing his uncle Mattaniah on the throne and changing his name to Zedekiah (vs. 17).

Zedekiah's Reign; the Fall of the Kingdom (24:18—25:21)

A great deal of light is thrown upon the events of the reign, especially during the siege, and upon the character of the king by certain narratives in the Book of Jeremiah (see Jer. 21:1-10; 24; 27; 28; 29; 32; 34; 37-39; 49:34-39; 51:59-64). From the account of Jeremiah's relationship with him one would judge that Zedekiah was a well-meaning but weak man, who was finally brought to disaster by yielding, almost against his will, to the aggressive designs of the pro-Egyptian party at the court. The policy of rebellion was vigorously opposed by Jeremiah. The patience of the Babylonians had been exhausted by the previous rebellion, so this time, after a frightful siege lasting eighteen months, they determined to eliminate Judah as a source of resistance by ending the monarchy, destroying the capital city, and depopulating the land. Chapter 25:1-21 describes the measures they took. (The brief statement in verses 2-3 regarding the famine which resulted from the siege is horribly illuminated by the more extended, poetic account in Lamentations 4:1-20.) Verses 4-7 tell of the king's attempt to escape when the walls were breached, his capture at Jericho, and the inhuman torture to which he was subjected by Nebuchadrezzar at Riblah in Syria.

Verses 18-21 describe the execution, also at Riblah, of the leaders of the rebellion, the chief officials of church and state. Verses 8-10 and 13-17 tell of the despoiling of the Temple, the destruction of its fabric, and the razing of all the important buildings in Jerusalem, while verses 11 and 12 describe the carrying into exile of all except the poorest members of the populace. (The figures given in Jeremiah 52:28-30 suggest that the depopulation may have been somewhat less drastic than one would suppose from the present passage. It is also interesting to read of Jeremiah's own adventures at this time, in Jeremiah 40:1-6.) Thus the Books of Kings, which began with the rise to power of "Solomon in all his glory," end, for all practical purposes, with a picture of the daughter of Zion in the ashes of her grandeur, crying out,

> "Is it nothing to you, all you who pass by?
>   Look and see
>   if there is any sorrow like my sorrow" (Lam. 1:12).

Verse 21 was probably the original conclusion of the second edition of Kings, 25:22-30 having been added as an appendix some years later.

APPENDIX: EVENTS DURING THE EXILE

II Kings 25:22-30

The Governorship of Gedaliah (25:22-26)

With the monarchy gone, the Babylonians entrusted the governorship of Judah to Gedaliah, a high-principled Jewish gentleman whose father, Ahikam, had been sympathetic to Jeremiah (Jer. 26:24). (A seal inscribed with the name of this Gedaliah was found some years ago in the excavation of Lachish.) Gedaliah's headquarters were at Mizpah, a few miles north of Jerusalem. (At Tell en-Nasbeh, which may be Mizpah, there was found a seal of "Ja-azaniah," possibly the same person whose name occurs in verse 23 and in Jeremiah 40:8.) The spirit of rebellion, however, still seethed in certain small groups among the people, and Gedaliah was assassinated by Ishmael, a member of the Judean royal family. Terrified at the prospect of Babylonian vengeance, a considerable body of citizens emigrated to

Egypt. A detailed contemporary account of these events may be found in Jeremiah 40:7—44:30.

Jehoiachin Restored to Favor (25:27-30)

The wonder of the Bible story is that, out of disaster, faith in God was always able to create new hope. The person who added the little appendix to Kings (25:22-30) did so because he saw, in a comparatively insignificant event which occurred about twenty-five years after the fall of Jerusalem, what seemed to him the first sign that God's favor was beginning to turn once again toward his people. Jehoiachin, the next to the last king of Judah, was a captive in Babylon for thirty-seven years, but in the year 561 B.C. the Babylonian king released him from his confinement and gave him a place of honor in the royal court. There must have been many faithful Jews in Babylon to whom this seemed a bright omen of the future—the first faint glimmer of the dawn after a long, dark night. The sign was partially fulfilled when the Babylonian Exile came to an end (Ezra 1:1-3). Christians, however, will not hesitate to find the ultimate fulfillment of Israel's hope in the coming of Jesus Christ, who, according to one of the Gospels at least, was a descendant of this same Jehoiachin (see Matthew 1:12, where he is called, in Greek fashion, "Jechoniah").

OUTLINE

From Adam to Saul: Genealogical Lists. I Chronicles 1:1—9:44

The United Monarchy. I Chronicles 10:1—II Chronicles 9:31
  The Death of Saul (I Chron. 10:1-14)
  The Reign of David (I Chron. 11:1—29:30)
  The Reign of Solomon (II Chron. 1:1—9:31)

The History of Judah in the Time of the Divided Kingdoms.
II Chronicles 10:1—36:21
  The Reign of Rehoboam (II Chron. 10:1—12:16)
  The Reign of Abijah (II Chron. 13:1-22)
  The Reign of Asa (II Chron. 14:1—16:14)
  The Reign of Jehoshaphat (II Chron. 17:1—20:37)
  The Reign of Jehoram (II Chron. 21:1-20)
  The Reign of Ahaziah (II Chron. 22:1-9)
  The Reign of Athaliah (II Chron. 22:10—23:21)
  The Reign of Joash (II Chron. 24:1-27)
  The Reign of Amaziah (II Chron. 25:1-28)
  The Reign of Uzziah (II Chron. 26:1-23)
  The Reign of Jotham (II Chron. 27:1-9)
  The Reign of Ahaz (II Chron. 28:1-27)
  The Reign of Hezekiah (II Chron. 29:1—32:33)
  The Reign of Manasseh (II Chron. 33:1-20)
  The Reign of Amon (II Chron. 33:21-25)
  The Reign of Josiah (II Chron. 34:1—35:27)
  The Reign of Jehoahaz (II Chron. 36:1-4)
  The Reign of Jehoiakim (II Chron. 36:5-8)
  The Reign of Jehoiachin (II Chron. 36:9-10)
  The Reign of Zedekiah (II Chron. 36:11-21)

Appendix: Cyrus' Decree for Rebuilding the Temple.
II Chronicles 36:22-23

COMMENTARY

FROM ADAM TO SAUL: GENEALOGICAL LISTS
I Chronicles 1:1—9:44

Since First and Second Chronicles (except for the lists in I Chronicles 1-9 and the extract from Ezra in II Chronicles 36: 22-23) cover the same ground as I Samuel 31—II Samuel 24 and I-II Kings—and considerable parts of those books are repeated almost verbatim in Chronicles—the basic information given in the commentaries on Samuel and Kings will not be repeated here. In connection with every section, the portion of Samuel and Kings which is parallel to it will be noted so the reader may refer easily to the more extended discussion in the relevant comment. This should be done in every instance. The comment on Chronicles itself will be concerned only with the additions, omissions, and other alterations which are the distinctive contribution of "the Chronicler" (see Introduction).

The average reader will, admittedly, find very little profit in the reading of the lists in I Chronicles 1-9, although they have considerable value for the student of Israel's history. While the Chronicler's main interest was in the story of the people of Judah (and especially in the history of the Temple) from the time of David down to the days of Nehemiah (I Chron. 10—Neh. 13), he wished his readers to see this story in the perspective of world history, so he prefaced the narrative parts of his work with a series of genealogical tables showing how the Hebrew nation could trace its ancestry back to remotest times—even to Adam, the first member of the human race (1:1). The Chronicler's concern with genealogy is not, therefore, evidence of narrow vision and lack of imagination, but rather the contrary. He refused to tell the story of his people as though they were a small, isolated, self-contained group. For him, the national history of Israel was the climactic point in the history of the entire human race, and the building of the Temple—the place where God chose to manifest his glorious Presence—was the most important event that had ever occurred. The prefacing of the book by these genealogies is the author's method of setting in its proper context the story which follows.

We still need the Chronicler's sense of the grand sweep of

human history and of the purpose of God which runs through it. None of us are merely creatures of today; we are the product of generation after generation of men who have gone before us; through our affairs there still sweep tides of influence which first began to move in remote antiquity. Our lives gain enormously in depth and meaning when we see our small existence as part of the whole adventure of man upon earth. They gain especially if we see, as the Chronicler did, that any particular generation represents just one chapter in the onmoving purpose of God. We shall probably not wish to study these chapters in much detail, but even to look over them, with their long lists of sonorous ancient names, is to get some feeling for the debt which every period in human history owes to the innumerable generations which preceded it. It is interesting to note that the New Testament begins in much the same way (Matt. 1:1-17), with a genealogy reaching back to the time of Abraham, thus clearly setting the life and work of Jesus Christ within the context of the long history which had gone before.

Chapter 1 gives the traditional genealogies of the various nations of the then known world down to the time of Jacob. For the more detailed history of those faraway days the author knew his readers could consult the Book of Genesis from which these lists are taken. In chapter 2, the author begins the genealogy of the people of Israel, although one quickly perceives that he is really concerned only with Judah (2:3—4:23)—which included David and his descendants (ch. 3)—and with Simeon (4:24-43) and Benjamin (8:1-40). These three were the tribes which traditionally occupied the territory of the Southern Kingdom. The other tribes are dealt with in chapters 5-7 (those in Transjordan in chapter 5 and those of the north in chapter 7). This section also contains the genealogy of the tribe of Levi (ch. 6), to which the Chronicler presumably belonged and in which he had a special interest. Finally, chapter 9 contains a list of the inhabitants of postexilic Jerusalem and its ecclesiastical officials (vss. 1-34), to which there has been appended a list of the ancestors of Saul (vss. 35-44, repeated from 8:29-38) in order to provide a fitting introduction to the story of Saul which immediately follows.

In 7:6 "Zebulon" should be read instead of "Benjamin."

THE UNITED MONARCHY

I Chronicles 10:1—II Chronicles 9:31

The Death of Saul (10:1-14)

The Chronicler really begins his story with the accession of David to the throne, but he must tell the last episode of Saul's life in order to provide a background for it. The story is repeated almost verbatim from I Samuel 31, except for two significant changes. In verse 6 he changes the words "all his men" (I Sam. 31:6) to "all his house" (that is, his family), thus simplifying the history of the kingdom and making it unnecessary to tell of the struggle David had with Saul's feeble heir, Ish-bosheth (II Sam. 1-4), a story which seemed to him an irrelevant and distracting episode in David's triumphant, divinely ordained progress to the throne. At the end the Chronicler adds his own moral judgment upon the tragic career of Saul (vss. 13-14). To his mind, the death of Saul was a divine act of judgment, not the suicide of a defeated, unhappy human being.

The Reign of David (11:1—29:30)

David Acquires the Kingdom and a Capital (11:1-9)

Because David is the Chronicler's great hero, he will not allow his readers to hear of any event which might cast doubt upon David's clear title to the throne. Chronicles contains no suggestion that David had ever had any previous intimate relationship with the family of Saul or that he was for seven years king over Judah alone, during part of which time he was engaged in a sanguinary conflict with the remnant of Saul's dynasty. Therefore the author omits all of I Samuel 16-30 and II Samuel 1-4, as well as the summary in II Samuel 5:5. In his account David is spontaneously acclaimed king by the whole of Israel in obedience to a divine command (vs. 3). On the other hand, and probably with good reason, the Chronicler gives to Joab the credit for the conquest of Jerusalem (vs. 6), an accomplishment which is obscured by the present difficult text of II Samuel 5:6-8.

David's Mighty Men (11:10-47)

The Chronicler transfers this list from its position as an ap-

pendix to II Samuel (23:8-39) and integrates it into his account
of David's reign, giving the warriors a part in the coronation
(vs. 10) and adding some names not found in Samuel (vss.
41b-47).

Lists of the Adherents of David (12:1-40)

This chapter has no real parallel in Samuel, though verses
1-22 are set in the context of the narrative related in I Samuel
27:2-6. The Chronicler's intent is to glorify David by showing
that he was supported by "a great army" (vs. 22) of representatives from the tribes of Israel rather than just by a few hundred
malcontents as in I Samuel 22:2 and 27:2. Living more than 700
years after the events, the Chronicler could not conceive that
David had ever been regarded with anything less than the unani-
mous and almost mystical veneration which later generations
felt for him. Verses 1-22 name those who were supposedly
associated with David in the days of his exile; verses 23-40, those
who assisted in his coronation.

David Brings the Ark to Jerusalem (13:1—16:43)

David is the Chronicler's hero; the Temple is his center of interest. He brings the two together by showing, first, how David
brought the Ark to Jerusalem (chs. 13-16), and then how he prepared for the building of a Temple to house it (chs. 21-29). In
describing the advent of the Ark he makes use of the valuable
account in II Samuel 6 and merely expands it by filling in the
details with information drawn from Temple customs of his own
day. In doing this he is following the procedure later adopted by
the painters of the Renaissance, who portrayed the characters
of the Bible as clothed in Renaissance dress and acting their
roles in Italian or Flemish landscapes. What we learn from his
additions to the narrative has little value for understanding the
reign of David, but it is of great importance for the light it casts
on worship in the Temple in the time of the Chronicler.

The Chronicler's own introduction to the story of the Ark
appears in 13:1-5. As would be expected, he transforms the
relatively simple ceremonies of II Samuel 6 into an elaborate
ecclesiastical procession (notice the mention of priests and Levites in vs. 2), and emphasizes, far beyond anything found in
Samuel, the participation of "all Israel" from far south to utter-
most north (vs. 5). Verses 6-14 repeat, with only slight differ-

ences, the story told in II Samuel 6:2-11, including the curious
incident of the death of Uzzah (vs. 10), which caused David to
interrupt the progress of the Ark and leave it for a while in the
home of Obed-edom (vss. 13-14).

The Chronicler's tendency to exalt the piety of David is shown
by the way in which he inserts at this point (ch. 14) the material
of II Samuel 5:11-25, which tells first of all (II Sam. 5:11-16)
how David built his palace and enlarged his harem. In Second
Samuel this story is related *before* the bringing of the Ark into
the city. The Chronicler finds it inconceivable that David should
have been concerned to build his own house before making plans
for the House of the Lord, and so he transfers the account of
these events (I Chron. 14:1-7) to a point *after* David had taken
the first steps toward bringing the Ark to Jerusalem. The story of
David's war with the Philistines (II Sam. 5:17-25) is similarly
relegated to a position of secondary importance. In Chronicles,
David tends to become a purely religious and even ecclesiastical
figure rather than the warrior and successful politician of the
narrative in the Books of Samuel.

The story of David's preparations for the final stage of the
Ark's movements toward Jerusalem (15:1-24) is without any
parallel whatsoever in Samuel. The lack of success which attended
the previous effort is explained as due to David's failure to let
the Levites exercise their proper function as bearers of the Ark
(vs. 2), and the death of Uzzah is interpreted in the same way
(vs. 13). Determined not to make the same mistake again, David
is represented as arranging to be assisted by the various Levitical
guilds (this is the meaning of the phrase "sons of" in verses
5-10) as well as by the priests (vs. 11). The Chronicler's particular interest in music (he was probably a Temple singer himself)
is shown in verses 16-22. There is mention of three guilds of
Levitical singers, Heman, Asaph, and Ethan (compare the titles
of Psalms 50, 73-83, 88, 89). The passage also includes two
mysterious technical terms relating to ancient Hebrew music,
"Alamoth" (vs. 20; compare Ps. 46, title) and "Sheminith"
(vs. 21; compare Ps. 6, title). With some significant changes,
15:25—16:3 reproduces II Samuel 6:12-19. David's conduct is
pictured as somewhat more dignified (compare vs. 27 with II
Sam. 6:14), and there is only incidental reference (vs. 29) to
his unhappy conflict with Michal, his wife (compare II Samuel
6:16, 20-23). In 16:4 the Chronicler resumes his own account of

the musical accompaniments of the ceremony and even includes the words—taken from the Psalter—of the anthems he believes they might have sung (vss. 8-22, compare Ps. 105:1-15; vss. 23-33, compare Ps. 96; vss. 34-36, compare Ps. 106:1, 47-48). Only at the end does he return to the text of Samuel (vs. 43; compare II Sam. 6:19b-20a).

David's Intention to Build a Temple (17:1-27)

Since David was his great hero, the Chronicler found it difficult to understand why he did not immediately go on to build the Temple after bringing the Ark into his capital city and why, instead, he left this important task to be performed by his son. The question was not a new one, and the author found in the Books of Samuel (II Sam. 7) a partial answer to it—namely, that David had *wished* to build the Temple, but was prohibited from doing so by a direct revelation from God through the prophet Nathan. So the Chronicler included this account, which also contained a pledge of permanence for the Davidic dynasty (I Chron. 17:12; II Sam. 7:13) in his own narrative with hardly any alteration. Later on he will give what he understands to be the reason for the prohibition, that is, that David was primarily a man of war (22:8; 28:3) and will tell how David made all the necessary preparations for the building (chs. 21-29).

David's Victories in War (18:1-17)

This chapter, which tells of David's success in extending his rule over the Philistines (vss. 1-2), the Syrians (vss. 3-11), and the Edomites (vss. 12-13), and lists the major officials of his court (vss. 14-17), is copied almost verbatim from II Samuel 8. In two places the Chronicler obviously had a more intelligible text before him than is found in our present Books of Samuel: in verse 1, he reads "Gath and its villages" instead of the mysterious "Metheg-ammah" of II Samuel 8:1; and in verse 12 he has, correctly, "Edomites" instead of the "Syrians" of the Hebrew of II Samuel 8:13 (see margin). He also removes the reference to David's cruel treatment of the Moabites (compare 1 Chron. 18:2 with II Sam. 8:2) and, in accordance with the strict view of the priesthood current in his own day, makes David's sons royal officials (vs. 17) instead of "priests" (II Sam. 8:18).

David's War with Ammon (19:1—20:8)

Because of his contention that Saul's entire family had perished at the battle of Gilboa (see 10:6), the Chronicler may have felt compelled to omit the attractive story in II Samuel 9 which tells of David's kindness to the son of Jonathan. He also omitted the entire account of David's immoral relationship with Bathsheba (II Sam. 11:2—12:25), but included the story of his war with the Ammonites (which, in Samuel, provides the framework for the Bathsheba episode) in order to complete the list of David's victories. Verse 1 of chapter 20 through the phrase " . . . remained at Jerusalem" parallels II Samuel 11:1; for the last sentence of the verse the Chronicler skips to II Samuel 12:26. ("Rabbah" is the modern city of Amman, capital of the Kingdom of Jordan.) Verses 2 and 3 of chapter 20 repeat II Samuel 12:30-31, with only slight differences.

Following the policy of omitting everything unfavorable to David, the Chronicler now passes over entirely the fascinating narrative of Absalom's revolt against his father (II Sam. 13-19), the rebellion of the northern tribes under the leadership of Sheba (II Sam. 20), David's unheroic sacrifice of part of Saul's family to the vengeance of the Gibeonites (II Sam. 21:1-14), and his undignified weakness in a battle with the Philistines (II Sam. 21:15-17). This brings the Chronicler to II Samuel 21:18-22, which he reproduces in I Chronicles 20:4-8. The principal change he introduces is to make Elhanan the slayer of "Lahmi the brother of Goliath" in order to remove the contradiction between II Samuel 21:19 and I Samuel 17 as to the identity of Goliath's killer. Omitting the poetry in II Samuel 22:1—23:7, and the list of David's associates in war (II Sam. 23:8-39) which he has already used in 11:10-41a, the Chronicler now comes to the story of the ill-advised census, which provides him with a good introduction to the account of David's preparations for the building of the Temple.

David's Preparations for the Temple (21:1—22:19)

As David's first act after becoming king was to bring the Ark up to Jerusalem (chs. 13-16), so his latter days, according to the Chronicler, were spent in making elaborate preparations for the building of the Temple, which would then be completed, with a minimum of effort, by his son Solomon. Once again we see how, in the Chronicler's mind, David's significance was religious, rather than political or military. There is, of course, no trace of this kind of activity in the original narrative in Samuel. The Chronicler uses II Samuel 24 because it seemed to tell how the site for the Temple was chosen, but the rest of the story is the product of the author's devotion to the Temple and its worship; he knew what he would have done if he had been king, and he could not imagine that David did otherwise.

He makes several interesting and apparently deliberate changes in the story as told in II Samuel 24. Since, quite rightly, he could not believe that God himself ever tempts men to commit sin, he changed the subject of the verb in II Samuel 24:1 from "the Lord" to "Satan." This is the only place in the Old Testament where Satan is pictured as a figure, independent of God, who tempts men to sin. Elsewhere "the satan"—that is, "the adversary"—is merely a servant of God appointed to act as a kind of celestial prosecuting attorney (see Job 1:6; Zech. 3:1). In several verses the author also introduces an angel where one does not appear, or is at least less conspicuous, in the text of Samuel (compare 21:11-12, 18, 20, and 27 with their parallels in II Samuel 24:13, 18, 20, 25); in verse 16 he gives an awesome description of the angel (compare II Sam. 24:17). These changes are due to the Chronicler's high conception of God, who, according to his view, must not be thought of as directly involved in the ugly things which take place upon the earth. While the Chronicler's treatment of history sometimes makes the modern reader feel a little uncomfortable, there can be no doubt that his theology is of a very high order. His God is no petty tribal deity, but the majestic and uncorruptible Lord of the universe.

In the first verse of chapter 22 the author makes it clear why he decided to make use of this rather curious story from II Samuel. The threshing floor of Ornan (called "Araunah" in II Samuel) was the divinely indicated spot on which the new Temple was to be built. This entire chapter has no parallel in the older and more historical narrative of Samuel. First of all, the Chronicler represents David as assembling all the materials that would be needed in the building of the Temple (vss. 2-5). Then David summons Solomon, explains to him that he cannot build the Temple himself because his hands have shed too much blood, and instructs Solomon to build it after his death with the materials he has provided (vss. 6-16). The point of verse 9 is that the very name "Solomon" is derived from the Hebrew word for "peace." Finally, the king commands all his officials to assist Solomon in performing the task he has just given him (vss. 17-19).

David's Final Arrangements (23:1—29:30)

These chapters have no parallel in Second Samuel or First Kings and give an impression of the events marking the last days of David which is different from the one found in those books. There is no trace in the Chronicler of the wretched intrigues which plagued the court during the old king's final illness and which finally brought Solomon to the throne (I Kings 1). In the Chronicler's version David simply appoints Solomon as his successor and spends the rest of his time making arrangements for the dignified ordering of the Temple services (chs. 23-26) and for the military and civil administration of the kingdom (ch. 27). His last act is to conduct a great national assembly (chs. 28-29), at which he announces that Solomon is to build the Temple (ch. 28) and solemnly dedicates the offerings made for the purpose by himself and his nobles (29:1-22).

Chapter 23 describes how David organized the Levites to assist in the work of the Temple. Since the Chronicler was presumably a Levite himself, this section no doubt contains authentic information about the organization and duties of the Levites in his own time. Verses 6-27 tell how they were divided into three groups, Gershonites, Kohathites, and Merari-ites, while verses 28-32 describe their duties as assistants to the priests.

Chapter 24 tells of the arrangements for the priests ("the sons of Aaron"). They are mentioned after the Levites because they are a subdivision of the tribe of Levi. There were two great families of priests, that of Eleazar and that of Ithamar (vs. 2). Altogether they were divided into twenty-four sections, each of which took its turn of duty in the Temple (vss. 7-19; compare vs. 10 with Luke 1:5, 8-9). Verses 20-31 contain an additional list of Levites; why the list should be introduced at this point is not known.

Chapter 25 deals with a special group of Levites who constituted the Temple choirs. This was apparently the group to which the Chronicler himself belonged, to judge by the interest in liturgical music which is so prominent a feature of his work (see 15:16-22; 16:4-42; II Chron. 5:12-13; 29:27-30; Ezra 3: 10-11; Neh. 12:27). There were three guilds of musicians:

Asaph, Heman, and Jeduthun ("Ethan" in 15:17). Like the priests, they were divided into twenty-four sections (vss. 9-31). The word "prophesy" used of their singing (vs. 1) reminds us of the ancient connection between music and the trances of the prophets (I Sam. 10:5-6; II Kings 3:15). Originally groups of prophets were probably attached to all the sanctuaries; the guilds of Levitical singers represent the later, crystallized development of these prophetic communities.

Chapter 26 tells of Levites who had still other functions: keepers of the Temple gates (vss. 1-19); guardians of the Temple treasuries (vss. 20-28); and representatives of the Temple in external affairs such as the collection of taxes (vss. 29-32).

Chapter 27 describes the organization of the army into twelve groups, each with its monthly turn of duty (vss. 1-15), and lists the chief civil officials of the various tribes (vss. 16-24), the administrators who performed certain special functions (vss. 25-31), and the members of the royal cabinet (vss. 32-34).

Finally, the Chronicler tells of a national assembly called by David to hear his final charge and to make a suitable contribution toward the building of the Temple (chs. 28-29). David explains that his own character as a warrior precluded him from building the Temple, Solomon his son being the divinely chosen instrument to carry out the task (28:2-8). Verses 9 and 10, as well as 20 and 21, addressed directly to Solomon, advise him to be loyal to God and faithful in fulfilling the purpose for which he will come to the throne. In verses 11-19, David delivers to Solomon the blueprints and specifications for the Temple and its worship which had been given to him by divine revelation (vs. 19), as the plan of the Tabernacle in the wilderness had once been given to Moses (Exod. 25:9). David then urges the nobles to follow his own example of generous giving and make a suitable contribution toward the house of God (29:1-5). The account of how this was done is found in verses 6-9, which is then followed by a truly beautiful prayer of dedication offered by the king (vss. 10-19). The mention of God's fatherhood in verse 10 is significant for the theology of the Chronicler, as is the reference to God's universal kingdom in the following verse. Verse 11 and the latter part of verse 14 are often used in Christian worship as "offertory sentences." The whole composition is an excellent illustration of the Chronicler's high conception of God and of man's proper relationship to him, and it exhibits a sensitive appreciation of

the art of public prayer. The concluding acts of the assembly
are described in verses 20-22a, with characteristic emphasis upon
the *joy* of worship (vs. 22). The book comes to an end with a
brief note on Solomon's accession (vss. 22b-25) and a summary
of David's reign (vss. 26-30), including an interesting list of
the sources available for the study of the reign (vs. 29). These
probably represent various sections of the present Books of
Samuel rather than independent documents.

The Reign of Solomon (II Chron. 1:1—9:31)

Introductory Statement (1:1-17)

In accordance with his usual practice of purifying Israel's history, the Chronicler omits the story of the sordid plots which
preceded Solomon's rise to power (I Kings 1-2) and proceeds
immediately to the story of his vision at the shrine at Gibeon.
In order to explain how Solomon could apparently have violated
the Deuteronomic law which prohibited sacrificial worship outside Jerusalem, the Chronicler supposes that the ancient Mosaic
Tabernacle was at that time temporarily housed at Gibeon
(vs. 3). The narrative of the king's prayer and God's response
is considerably abbreviated from that in First Kings, and the
illustrative story of the two harlots (I Kings 3:16-28) is omitted
entirely, perhaps because of its slightly unsavory tone. Because
he wishes to get as quickly as possible to the building of the
Temple, the author also omits the whole account of Solomon's
secular activities found in I Kings 4 and leaves the story of his
negotiations with Hiram of Tyre (I Kings 5:1-14) to be dealt
with in radically altered form in the next chapter (2:3-16).

The Building of the Temple (2:1—4:22)

The author now comes, after the briefest possible introduction,
to the theme which is of chief interest to him: the building and
consecration of the Temple. Verse 1 of chapter 2 is by the
Chronicler himself; verse 2 is derived from I Kings 5:15-16,
while verses 3-16 are very roughly parallel to I Kings 5:1-14
and 7:13-14. With his usual theological sensitivity, the Chronicler makes it clear that the Temple is not God's *habitation*, but
merely the place where liturgical worship can be offered to him
(vs. 6). Solomon is represented as having asked at the beginning that Huram ("Hiram" in Kings) send him a skillful artisan

to assist in the beautification of the Temple. This fusion of two separate items in Kings shows the Chronicler's skill at streamlining the narrative. In verse 17, Solomon's levy for forced labor is said to have been limited to "aliens," quite contrary to the impression given in I Kings 5:13.

Chapter 3, which gives some account of the shape and furnishings of the Temple, represents a considerable abridgment of the information given in I Kings 6 and 7:15-22. In verse 1, the author, probably repeating an identification which had become traditional in his day, asserts that the place where the Temple was built was not only the threshing floor of Ornan ("Araunah" in II Samuel 24) the Jebusite (I Chron. 21:28—22:1) but was also Mount Moriah, where Abraham had once been willing to offer his only son as a sacrifice (Gen. 22:2).

Chapter 4 contains a shorter description of the furniture mentioned in I Kings 7. However, the Chronicler adds two items of information which are not found there: first (vs. 1), he includes mention of the bronze altar, which is omitted in I Kings 7 although it is referred to in II Kings 16:14; second (vs. 6), he tells what he conceives to be the function of the great "sea" and the lavers, that is, to serve as washbasins for cleansing.

The Dedication of the Temple (5:1—7:22)

While abbreviating the description of the Temple structure and its furnishings, the author characteristically expands the account of the ecclesiastical ceremonies connected with the dedication. First of all he describes how the Ark was brought up to the newly completed Temple, but between the first and second halves of I Kings 8:10 (II Chron. 5:11a and 13b) he inserts a paragraph dealing with the way in which the Levitical singers performed their function on this occasion. The reader will remember that the music of the Temple was the Chronicler's special focus of interest. Both vocal and instrumental music are mentioned, and the text of the Levitical doxology is given (II Chron. 5:13; compare Pss. 106:1; 118:1-4, 29; 136). He also names once more the guilds of Levitical singers (5:12; compare I Chron. 25:1). The Ark having been installed, King Solomon then begins his dedicatory prayer (II Chron. 6), which is repeated almost verbatim from I Kings 8:12-50. Since only priests were (in the author's time) allowed to stand before the altar, he adds to I Kings 8:22 the explanation that the king was not really usurping priestly rights but merely making use of a special platform or pulpit which had been placed for the purpose in front of the altar (vs. 13). He omits the last part of I Kings 8:50 and vss. 51-53—the rather limp conclusion of the prayer in its Deuteronomic version—and provides it with a far more stirring and liturgically artistic climax partly drawn from Psalm 132:8-9. Probably because the Chronicler conceived blessing to be a distinctively priestly function, he leaves out the item that Solomon blessed the congregation (I Kings 8:55-61) and substitutes, in II Chronicles 7:1-3, the information that fire from heaven came down and consumed the sacrifice, a dramatic manifestation of divine favor which immediately called forth the praises of the congregation.

The story of the dedication sacrifices is told in 7:4-10 (see I Kings 8:62-66) with a typical interpolation about the music performed on the occasion (vs. 6). The chapter concludes (vss. 11-22) with the vision which Solomon received after his work on the Temple was complete. Except for verses 13-15, which are added, the account follows very closely that of I Kings 9:1-9.

Miscellaneous Activities (8:1-18)

Throughout this section there are numerous alterations in the text of Kings, for reasons which are fairly obvious. Thus the cities which, in I Kings 9:10-14, were given by Solomon to Hiram in order to settle his debt are here said to have been given by Hiram to Solomon (vs. 2). First Kings has no mention of the military campaign against Hamath-zobah (vs. 3) or of the fortification of Upper Beth-horon and the building of numerous fortified cities (vs. 5; compare I Kings 9:17). The fact that Solomon obtained Gezer as a gift from his Egyptian father-in-law (I Kings 9:16) is passed over in silence, while the nearby and comparatively insignificant city of Tamar (I Kings 9:18) becomes the famous caravan city of Tadmor (Palmyra), northeast of Damascus (vs. 4). The damaging admission that the Israelites *could* not overcome all the older population of the land (I Kings 9:21) is softened to the statement that they *did* not (vs. 8). Solomon's arrangements for his Egyptian wife, which in I Kings 3:1 and 9:24 are merely a matter of personal convenience, are given a religious motivation in verse 11. Verses 14-16 are a typical addition by the Chronicler. Whereas Hiram, according to I Kings 9:27, sent *sailors* to Ezion-geber and Eloth on the Red Sea, the Chronicler shows some deficiency in geographical knowledge by having him send ships also (vs. 18)—long before the Suez Canal was built! The chapter is an instructive one for seeing how the Chronicler handled his sources.

The Queen of Sheba's Visit (9:1-12)

This is repeated almost without variation from I Kings 10: 1-13.

The Wealth of Solomon (9:13-28)

The only interesting variation from I Kings 10:14-29 is that the Chronicler's indifferent knowledge of geography led him to suppose that the Tarshish-*style* ships of I Kings 10:22 actually went from Solomon's Red Sea port to Tarshish in the western Mediterranean (vs. 21).

The Death of Solomon: Summary of His Reign (9:29-31)

The Chronicler attributes his information about the reign of Solomon to the histories of Nathan, Ahijah, and Iddo, although internal evidence seems to show that these are merely names for different parts of the First Book of Kings. It will be noted that he passes over altogether the discreditable tales of Solomon's relations with his foreign wives and the widespread dissatisfaction with his reign recorded in I Kings 11:1-40.

THE HISTORY OF JUDAH IN THE TIME OF THE DIVIDED KINGDOMS

II Chronicles 10:1—36:21

The Reign of Rehoboam (10:1—12:16)

Chapter 10 reproduces I Kings 12:1-19 almost without change, while 11:1-4 is taken almost verbatim from I Kings 12:21-24. First Kings 12:20, which tells of Jeroboam's coronation as king of Israel, is omitted because the Chronicler resolutely rejects anything which belongs properly to the history of the Northern Kingdom. The long section 11:5—12:8 consists of material which is found only in Chronicles and may be drawn from an independent source. Its historical value is much debated, but it may contain at least a certain amount of reliable information. This statement applies particularly to verses 5-12, which tell how the king strengthened the fortifications of a number of strategic sites and increased the efficiency of the country's organization for military defense. In verses 13-17 one can see more clearly the Chronicler's own theological tendencies at work in his statement that all the priests and Levites of the northern territories deserted Jeroboam and came down to settle in Judah. It is probable that the account of the various royal marriages in verses 18-23 comes from an independent and reliable source. A large part of 12:1-12, which tells of Shishak's invasion (I Kings 14:25-28), is devoted to explaining, on moral and theological grounds, how such a disaster could have occurred. It was because Rehoboam and his people "forsook the law of the LORD" (vss. 1, 5); only their repentance and humble submission to God's will prevented them from suffering an even worse fate (vss. 7-8).

The Reign of Abijah (13:1-22)

The portrait of Abijah in Chronicles is very different from that in I Kings 15:1-8 (where, incidentally, he is called "Abijam"). The Deuteronomic historian had nothing good to say about him, but in the Chronicler's account he has become an ardent protagonist of the true religion. The mention in I Kings (15:6-7) of hostilities between Abijah and Jeroboam has been expanded into the long account of a great victory won by Abijah (vss. 3-20), before which Abijah is reported to have delivered an eloquent speech contrasting the apostasy of Israel with the faithfulness of Judah (vss. 4-12). The Chronicler's version is said to be based upon a now lost book entitled "the story of the prophet Iddo" (vs. 22). The phrase "covenant of salt" in verse 5 means an indissoluble promise; the name arises from the fact that in the Semitic world the partaking together of "bread and salt" creates an unbreakable bond between the two parties concerned.

The Reign of Asa (14:1-16:14)

The account of the attack upon the south of Judah made by "Zerah the Ethiopian" and his miraculous defeat (14:9-15) has no parallel in Kings. It may of course be based upon some genuine reminiscence of a raid by Egyptians or Arabs. For the Chronicler the most important event in Asa's reign was the reform of worship which is described in five verses in Kings, but here occupies a whole chapter (ch. 15). The reformation is said to have been inspired by the preaching of an otherwise unknown prophet by the name of Azariah the son of Oded (vss. 1-8). The following verses (9-15) describe the summoning of a great national assembly at Jerusalem, similar to that which occurred in the reign of Josiah (II Kings 23), for the purpose of establishing a covenant of fidelity between the nation and its God. Only 14:2 and 15:16-18 are taken from Kings; the rest is the Chronicler's idealization of the events. Contrary to I Kings 15:16, which speaks of continual war between Judah and the Northern Kingdom, the Chronicler states that war between Asa and Baasha, the king of Israel, did not break out until Asa's thirty-sixth year (15:19; 16:1). The Chronicler passes a less favorable judgment on Asa than the older Book of Kings, roundly condemning him through the mouth of "Hanani the seer," for having made an alliance with the Syrians (16:7-10). No doubt the author understood the king's disease "in his feet" (16:12) to be a punishment for his lack of faith. Furthermore, he reports, the king, when sick, sought help from physicians rather than from God. His funeral rites are described as especially magnificent (vs. 14). The "very great fire" is not to be taken as referring to cremation (which the Hebrews did not practice), but probably to a ceremonial fire on which incense and spices were cast.

The Reign of Jehoshaphat (17:1—20:37)

The story of Jehoshaphat is recounted at much greater length in Chronicles than in I Kings 22, and for some of the additional material, at least in chapter 17, the Chronicler may have had access to good sources of information. Most important is the account of the measures he took for the military strengthening of his kingdom (vs. 2) and the building of fortresses and store cities (vs. 12). It is curious that the Chronicler, anxious to save the reputation of Jehoshaphat, in verse 6 deliberately alters the statement of I Kings 22:43 that "the high places were not taken away." No doubt he argued with himself that, in view of Jehoshaphat's well-known zeal, the statement in Kings must be erroneous.

Verses 7-9 speak of an organized attempt to teach the Law to all the people of the land. It seems more likely that this is a reflection of conditions in the Chronicler's own day—when Judaism was becoming increasingly a religion of the Law and its learned exponents—than that it is an accurate account of the growth of concern for religious education in the time of Jehoshaphat. Every historian has a natural tendency to describe the past in terms of his own present. The number of available soldiers in Judah is listed at 1,160,000 (vss. 14-19). This is obviously greatly exaggerated, as the Chronicler's numbers frequently are.

Chapter 18 reproduces I Kings 22:1-35 but incorporates the incident into the history of Judah, whereas in Kings it belongs to the history of Israel, and Ahab rather than Jehoshaphat is the central figure. This is the only extract from the history of the Northern Kingdom of which the Chronicler makes any use. The sequel at the beginning of chapter 19 (vss. 1-3), which tells how the king was rebuked by "Jehu the son of Hanani the seer" for having allied himself with the apostate Israelites, has no parallel in Kings. Verses 4-11 describe the organization of a judicial system throughout the country. It is difficult to know whether this account is based upon a reliable historical source outside of Kings, or whether, as some interpreters suggest, it is merely an inference drawn from the fact that the king's name means in Hebrew "The Lord has *judged*."

Second Kings 3:4-27 records an invasion of Moab which Jehoshaphat made as an ally of Jehoram, king of Israel, but does not include the events described in II Chronicles 20:1-30, where the Moabites and Ammonites are said to have invaded Judah and to have been miraculously defeated. Unlike the story in Kings, this one seems to bear the clear stamp of legend. The Chronicler's battle is an ecclesiastical affair in which the army is expressly told beforehand that it will not need to fight (vs. 17). The whole story is better taken as a kind of parable on man's need to trust in God than as the account of a historical event. Notable elements in it are the king's prayer (vss. 5-12), the oracle delivered by a Levite in the fashion of one of the old prophets (vss. 14-17), and the king's address before the "battle" (vs. 20) in which he uses a familiar passage from Isaiah (Isa. 7:9). Victory for the Hebrew armies is said to have come about as the result of internal conflict among the invaders (vs. 23).

So effectively did they destroy one another that all that was left for Jehoshaphat's forces was to plunder the bodies of the slain— a process which occupied no less than three days (vss. 24-25). Characteristic of the Chronicler's interests is the emphasis on the Levites and liturgical music (vss. 14, 19, 21, 28). The story of Jehoshaphat's reign comes to an end (vss. 35-37) with a somewhat altered version of I Kings 22:48 in which (as in II Chron. 9:21) the Tarshish-*type* ships of Kings become ships actually intended to go to Tarshish. The record in I Kings 22:49 indicates that Jehoshaphat refused to enter into an alliance with Ahaziah, whereas in the Chronicler's version the destruction of his merchant marine is said to have been a punishment for entering the alliance.

The Reign of Jehoram (21:1-20)

The Chronicler's account of the entire period covering the reigns of Jehoshaphat, Jehoram, and Ahaziah is greatly impoverished by the necessity of omitting the colorful and instructive Elijah-Elisha stories because these belong to the history of the Northern Kingdom, with which he refused to concern himself. Nevertheless, the author assumes that his readers know who Elijah was, since he mentions him without further introduction in this chapter as being, supposedly, the author of a letter to Jehoram. The letter denounced the king for following the example of the kings of Israel and predicted disaster for his family and death by a dreadful disease for himself (vss. 12-15). The disaster is described in verses 16-17 and the king's death in verses 18-20. None of this has any parallel in Kings (II Kings 8:16-24), nor do the introductory verses 2-4.

The Reign of Ahaziah (22:1-9)

Verses 1-6 reproduce substantially the narrative of II Kings 8: 25-29, correcting the matter of the king's age and placing greater emphasis upon the evil influence of the house of Ahab. Verses 7-9, however, which tell the story of Ahaziah's assassination, differ so much from the account in II Kings 9:27-28 that they must be based upon some other source.

The Reign of Athaliah (22:10—23:21)

This narrative is in the main a repetition of the story in II Kings 11, with a few additions and some alteration of details. Thus the Chronicler adds that Jeho-shabe-ath (in Kings "Jehosheba") was not only Ahaziah's sister but the wife of the priest Jehoiada, who was the author of the plot against Athaliah. In 23:1-3 the palace conspiracy described in Kings, in which foreign mercenaries (the Carites) played an important part, becomes, rather improbably, a great national and ecclesiastical movement involving the Levites (note the introduction of the Levites in verses 4-8 also). The Chronicler may have found it impossible to believe that foreigners would have played such a role or even have been admitted to the Temple courts.

The Reign of Joash (24:1-27)

The story of Joash (called "Jehoash" in II Kings 12:1) and his plan to repair the Temple (vss. 4-14) is based upon II Kings 12:4-16 but has been rewritten by the Chronicler to accord better with his ideas of what was fitting and proper—especially with regard to the work of the priests, who do not appear in a very favorable light in Kings (compare vs. 5 with the blunt statement of II Kings 12:6). The Chronicler tells also about the death of Jehoiada (vs. 15), which is said to have provided the partisans of religious syncretism with an opportunity once more to gain power in the court (vss. 17-19). When Zechariah, the son and successor of Jehoiada, publicly protested against the king's reactionary policy, he was stoned to death, at the king's orders, right in the Temple court (vss. 20-22). It is probably this murder that is referred to in Luke 11:51, where the point is that these were the first and last murders described in the Hebrew Bible. The murder of Abel occurs in Genesis, the first book (Gen. 4:8); the murder of Zechariah is narrated in II Chronicles, the last book of the *Hebrew* Old Testament. (See the comment on II Chronicles 36:22-23 for an explanation of this curious fact about the arrangement of the Hebrew Bible.) In Matthew 23:35 the victim of this murder is called Zechariah "the son of Barachiah," that is, the *prophet* Zechariah, but this is almost certainly the result of an ancient error.

The apostasy of Joash and the brutal murder of his chief priest provided, in the Chronicler's mind, the necessary theological and moral explanation of the king's later defeat by the Syrians (vss. 23-24) and his subsequent assassination (vss. 25-26). We are thus reminded once more of the Chronicler's belief that God is absolutely just and that he demands complete loyalty and obedience from his servants. The Chronicler's purpose in writing history was not so much to restate the cold facts of history as to make his readers conscious of their relationship to God and of all that this implies.

The Reign of Amaziah (25:1-28)

The Chronicler follows the main outline of the brief account of Amaziah's reign in II Kings 14, but with considerable and characteristic additions. In verses 1-4 he follows closely II Kings 14:2-6 but omits verse 4. One verse in Kings (14:7) becomes nine verses in Chronicles (vss. 5-13). Amaziah is said to have hired mercenary troops from Israel to assist him in his war with Edom but to have been dissuaded from using them by the influence of an unnamed prophet. The author reports that after the capture of the Edomite stronghold, 10,000 of the enemy's soldiers were hurled from the top of "the rock"—a well-known, almost inaccessible plateau, surrounded by high cliffs, located near the site of ancient Petra. After these events Amaziah, it is said, apostatized from the true religion of Israel despite the warning of a prophet (vss. 14-16), a fact which provided ample theological justification for his subsequent defeat at the hands of Israel (vss. 17-24) and his eventual assassination (vss. 27-28).

The Reign of Uzziah (26:1-23)

It is probable that the account of Uzziah's victories (in Kings he is called "Azariah") found in verses 6-15, which have no parallel in the Deuteronomic history, is based upon at least a nucleus of sound historical information. What is known of Uzziah from the books of the prophets indicates that his time was one of unusual prosperity. The details which are given here of his successful wars with the Philistines and Arabs and of his building activities harmonize very well with that picture. Especially interesting is the mention in verse 15 of the construction of war machines. In verses 16-23 the Chronicler explains that the leprosy of Uzziah (II Kings 15:5) was due to his presumptuous attempts to usurp the priestly function of offering incense at the Temple altar.

The Reign of Jotham (27:1-9)

The Chronicler adds little to the account in II Kings 15:32-38 beyond the fact that Jotham continued the aggressive policies of his father. He engaged in considerable building activity and subjugated the Ammonites (vss. 3-6).

The Reign of Ahaz (28:1-27)

For this reign the Chronicler follows the general outlines of the story in II Kings 16 but completely rewrites it so as to emphasize even more strongly the wickedness of the king and the magnitude of his defeats. The Syro-Ephraimite War (II Kings 16:5-6), which was an unsuccessful attempt to capture Jerusalem (Isa. 7:1), becomes in Chronicles two separate invasions permitted by God in order to punish the nation for the policies of its king (vss. 5-7). The calamitous results of Judah's defeat by the Northern Kingdom were mitigated only by the intervention of an Israelite prophet (vss. 8-15). Ahaz then summoned help from Assyria, not against the Syro-Ephraimite alliance, as in II Kings 16:7, but against invading Edomites and Philistines (vss. 16-19). This policy resulted only in further humiliation (vss. 20-21). Finally, instead of merely introducing Assyrian elements into the worship of the Lord (II Kings 16:10-16), Ahaz, it is said, became an active devotee of the gods of Damascus (vss. 22-25) and went so far as even to close the Temple (vs. 24).

The Reign of Hezekiah (29:1—32:33)

The greater part of the space allotted to Hezekiah's reign in Kings is taken up with a tremendously interesting account of Sennacherib's invasion (II Kings 18:13—19:37)—derived from some popular source—and with the closely related account of Hezekiah's illness (II Kings 20). The Chronicler compresses all of this material into 32:1-26. His own narrative is occupied chiefly with Hezekiah's ecclesiastical activities. Since Hezekiah

was a reforming king (see II Kings 18:3-6), the Chronicler felt
sure what course he must have followed. The Temple had been
closed and neglected since sometime in the reign of Ahaz
(28:24), so the new king's first act would necessarily be to open
and cleanse it and celebrate the occasion with proper ceremonies.
These are the events which are recounted in chapter 29. As is
to be expected, the Levites play a prominent part (vss. 4-5, 12,
34) and, in accordance with the Chronicler's special field of
interest, considerable emphasis is placed upon their rendition of
music appropriate to the occasion (vss. 25-30). Verse 30 is no
doubt a reference to the Psalms, which in the Chronicler's day
were being collected into our present Psalter.

Following the reopening of the Temple, Hezekiah is said to
have organized a unique celebration of the Passover (ch. 30),
to which not only the citizens of Judah but also the inhabitants
of the former kingdom of Israel, which had just recently been
destroyed by the Assyrians (vs. 6), were cordially invited by
letters sent from the king. Because the cleansing of the Temple
had not been completed by the proper date for the Passover
observance, advantage was taken of a law which permitted it to
be celebrated one month later (vss. 2-3; compare Num. 9:9-11).
Verses 13-27 describe the actual ceremonies. The culminating
act of this great festival was a thorough reformation of religious
abuses throughout the entire territory of Israel and Judah (31:1).

The third significant deed of Hezekiah is reported to have
been his reorganization of the system for the support of the clergy
(31:2-19)—to the great and understandable satisfaction of the
beneficiaries (vs. 10).

Chapter 32, the much abbreviated version of II Kings 18:13—
20:21, contains first of all the story of Sennacherib's invasion
(vss. 1-23), then the merest sketch of the events connected with
Hezekiah's illness (vss. 24-26), and finally a general summary of
his reign (vss. 27-33). The chapter contains two references to the
building of the Siloam tunnel (vss. 3-4 and 30), the latter of
which is much clearer than the account in II Kings 20:20. In
verse 19 we feel the deep sincerity of the author and his pas-
sionate concern for the glory and majesty of God when he
summarizes the speech of the Assyrian envoys in these horror-
filled words, "And they spoke of the God of Jerusalem as they
spoke of the gods of the peoples of the earth, which are the work
of men's hands."

The Reign of Manasseh (33:1-20)

For the Chronicler, as for the Deuteronomists who compiled the older Books of Kings, the fate of Manasseh presented a serious theological problem. He was the worst of the kings of Israel and yet had an unusually long and successful reign. The Deuteronomists were able to say no more than that the ultimate disaster which befell the kingdom was a tardy punishment for his wicked deeds. The Chronicler, however, was not satisfied with this explanation and supposes that Manasseh must at some time have undergone a change of heart. So to the account in II Kings 21: 1-18 he adds the story in verses 10-13—perhaps based upon an older tradition—that Manasseh was once carried captive to Assyria where he had opportunity for repentance and became a devout servant of the Lord (vss. 15-16). His captivity, if not his repentance, may well be historical. Verse 19 refers to his "prayer"; the little book in the Apocrypha called "The Prayer of Manasseh" is an attempt to guess its contents.

The Reign of Amon (33:21-25)

Chronicles adds nothing to the account in II Kings 21:19-26, beyond contrasting the wholly unregenerate character of Amon with that of his supposedly repentant father, Manasseh.

The Reign of Josiah (34:1—35:27)

According to the account in Kings (II Kings 22:3), the reforming activity of Josiah began in his eighteenth year, when the repair of the Temple began and "the book of the law" was found. In Chronicles, the king had already begun to manifest unusual piety in his eighth year, and in the twelfth year had initiated a thoroughgoing reformation (vss. 3-7) which finally *culminated* in the renovation of the Temple (vss. 8-13) and the discovery of the book of the Law (vss. 14-21). The finding of the book was not, therefore, the cause of the reformation (as in Kings) but only incidental to it.

In 35:1-19 there is an elaborate description of the Passover celebrated on this occasion, which was dealt with in only three verses in Kings (II Kings 23:21-23). The passage reveals once more the Chronicler's special interest in ecclesiastical ceremonies

and particularly in the Levites' part in them. The value of the
Chronicler's account of the death of Josiah in verses 20-24 as
supplementing and clarifying the account in Kings has already
been mentioned in the comment on II Kings 23:26-30. The
prophet Jeremiah, who curiously is not mentioned at all in Kings,
is appropriately introduced into the Chronicler's version of the
events, both here (vs. 25) and in the following chapter (36:
12, 21).

The Reign of Jehoahaz (36:1-4)

Concerning Jehoahaz there is no important difference here
from the account in II Kings 23:31-34.

The Reign of Jehoiakim (36:5-8)

The story in II Kings 23:35—24:7 knows nothing of the
imprisonment of Jehoiakim mentioned in verse 6 nor of the
despoiling of the Temple by Nebuchadrezzar in verse 7, although
the latter tradition was evidently familiar to the author of the
Book of Daniel (Dan. 1:1).

The Reign of Jehoiachin (36:9-10)

In II Kings 24:8, this king was said to have been eighteen at
his accession; here he is said to have been only eight. The account of his reign is drastically abridged (see II Kings 24:8-17).

The Reign of Zedekiah (36:11-21)

Verses 12-21 are the Chronicler's own résumé of the fall of
Jerusalem, told in very general terms and with chief emphasis
on the theological meaning of the events (see II Kings 24:18—
25:21). God in his great mercy, the Chronicler says, had sent
his people a long succession of prophets to warn them of the
inevitable consequences of disloyalty and disobedience. When
they stubbornly persisted in their ways, he finally had no alternative except to inflict the punishment which their behavior deserved (vss. 15-16). The Books of Kings closed their story
when the Babylonian empire was still standing in its strength
(II Kings 25:27-30). The Chronicler, who lived at least two

centuries later than the Deuteronomists who edited Kings, is able to conclude this part of his story with a reference to the eventual rise of Persia, which destroyed the Babylonian empire and brought the Babylonian Exile to an end (vs. 20). He sees the Exile as lasting seventy years in accordance with the words of Jeremiah the prophet (Jer. 25:11; 29:10). This was the period from the destruction of the Temple in 587 B.C. to its rebuilding in 515 B.C. During this period, he says somewhat ironically, the desolated land of Israel enjoyed all the sabbatical years ("its sabbaths") which its inhabitants had failed to observe during the preceding centuries (vs. 21; see Lev. 25:1-7; compare Lev. 26:27-28, 32-35).

APPENDIX: CYRUS' DECREE FOR REBUILDING THE TEMPLE

II Chronicles 36:22-23

These verses, which take up the story of the people of Israel where the Books of Kings had dropped it, are really no part of Second Chronicles. They are the opening two and a half verses of the Book of Ezra, which tells of Israel's return from exile and of the rebuilding of the Temple. They are put here in order to indicate the continuity of the story. As the books are arranged in the English Bible, where Ezra immediately follows Chronicles, they are unnecessary. In the Hebrew Bible, however, where Ezra and Nehemiah are printed *before* Chronicles, this device was a clever indication to the reader that he must turn back now to Ezra for the rest of the history. The reason for the strange and illogical arrangement of the books in the Hebrew canon is that Ezra and Nehemiah, which related a story without parallel in any other book of the Bible, were the first part of the Chronicler's work to be accepted as Holy Scripture. First and Second Chronicles were at first ignored because they merely retold the story which appeared in Kings and in some details contradicted it. Later on they, too, were accepted, but then they were simply tacked on to the end of the Bible, out of their natural order. So Second Chronicles is the *last* book in the Hebrew canon of Scripture (see the comment on II Chron. 24:1-27).

These facts remind us that First and Second Chronicles are not particularly important by themselves, except for the incidental light they throw upon the mind and times of the writer and a few stray bits of information which for one reason or another do not appear in Kings. Their greatest importance is in providing the author's own introduction to the third and fourth volumes of his great work, the books we call Ezra and Nehemiah. The Book of Ezra picks up the thread of narrative which was broken at the end of Second Kings. Its story of the return of the exiles and the reconstitution of Israel's national life on her own soil provides dramatic confirmation of the faith in God's good will toward his people which is expressed in the closing verses of II Kings 25. The ultimate confirmation of this faith is, of course, to be found in the New Testament, which tells how God, through the work of Jesus Christ, redeemed his people out of the *spiritual* exile which began in the Garden of Eden.